# JACOBS FIELD

# FIELD

## HISTORY & TRADITION AT THE JAKE

• VINCE McKEE •

FOREWORDS BY KENNY LOFTON, CHARLES NAGY AND JIM THOME

THE
History
PRESS

Published by The History Press
Charleston, SC 29403
www.historypress.net

All facts in the book were provided by www.baseball-reference.com and the athletes themselves.

*Front cover*: Jacobs Field. *Courtesy of Fran Warmuth, Elsa Spinelli-DeLuca and Michelle Lang.*
*Back cover, top*: Bridge to the ballpark. *Courtesy of Annie Murphy Choquette.*
*Back cover, bottom right*: Jacobs Field. *Courtesy of Emily McKee.*

First published 2014

ISBN 978-1-5402-2475-0

Library of Congress CIP data applied for.

*This book is dedicated to Dick Jacobs and family. It was your faith in Cleveland that helped provide years of memories for many passionate fans, including myself.*

# CONTENTS

# FOREWORD

The city of Cleveland put me on the map as a baseball player; it really put me where I needed to be. Because of Cleveland, my name became synonymous with Cleveland Indian baseball. I appreciate what the fans and everyone did for me, and I felt like I reciprocated and did as much as I could for the city of Cleveland. The team has some great and loyal fans who always wanted a championship, and I tried my hardest to make that happen. I just appreciate all the love and support they gave me the entire time I was there, and they will be something I will treasure for the rest of my life.

*Kenny Lofton*

# FOREWORD

I was able to be successful because I had the backing of the fans in Cleveland. They gave us tremendous support, and I loved being a part of everything because the fans made it easier on us to perform. The fans helped us compete and do our jobs. The Indians are a great organization in a great town with a great fan base. I still enjoy the memories. I try to get back to Cleveland often. I miss the fans, and every time I go back, it is a great time. I look forward to working with the Indians again because it was a fun place to play. I was very fortunate to be a part of it for so long. The city embraced my family and me. We had great neighbors who were very respectful to my entire family. I just wanted us to do well, work hard and win. The fans always showed us so much respect, and it helped me enjoy my time in Cleveland. I wouldn't trade my memories of Cleveland for anything else!

*Charles Nagy*

# A SPECIAL MESSAGE FROM JIM THOME

I want to say thanks for the memories and support. The fans came out every day, and I want to thank them for that. I hope that Cleveland will eventually win a world championship because the fans there deserve it. They have waited a long time, and I would love to see it happen.

*Jim Thome*

# ACKNOWLEDGEMENTS

I would like to thank my wife, Emily, and daughter, Maggie, for allowing me the time to write this book. I would like to thank Jim Friuglietti for his guidance on this project. A special thank-you to Curtis Danburg of the Cleveland Indians for once again going out of his way to help me out. I would like to thank my parents as well as my brother, Don, and sisters Abbie, Molly and Rebecca for always believing in me. A big thank-you to The History Press for working with me on this great story. Thank you to LaNasas Barbershop, Dr. Gosky and Richard Masci for supplying the bulk of the pictures. Most importantly, thank you to my lord and savior Jesus Christ—it is through his light that all work is done.

# INTRODUCTION

The sports landscape changed in the spring of 1994 when the Cleveland Indians moved into their new home at the corner of Carnegie and Ontario. No longer were they the joke of the league—their new home made them the jewel of baseball. Few could ever imagine that Jacobs Field would bring so many new and exciting memories. It has been twenty years of magic and winning the likes of which have never been seen before in our town. Fans and players around baseball will be the first to proclaim that there's no better place to play and watch a game than at "The Jake!"

Chapter 1

# A NEW ERA BEGINS

The most exciting time in the history of Cleveland baseball occurred between the 1994 and 1999 seasons, when the Cleveland Indians won five straight division titles. They won the American League pennant twice and even came within a few outs of winning the World Series. It all started years earlier when Richard Jacobs bought the team and envisioned what could happen if it played in a stadium that drew a good crowd. Jacobs's gamble paid off, as the new stadium would bear witness to a 455-game sellout streak.

Richard Jacobs bought the team in 1986 with his brother, David. At the time, the Indians were one of the worst teams in baseball. In addition to plans for new players and coaches, the new owner believed that a new stadium devoted exclusively to baseball would be needed. The Indians had been sharing Municipal Stadium with the Cleveland Browns.

In May 1990, the Cuyahoga County voters approved a fifteen-year "sin tax" on alcohol and cigarette sales to finance the new Gateway Sports and Entertainment Complex. Construction started eighteen months later, and the new era in Indians baseball began on the corner of Carnegie and Ontario in downtown Cleveland. The construction was completed in October 1993, just in time for the next spring's baseball season. The stadium cost nearly $175 million, with Jacobs funding over half of that. As baseball was set to begin in the spring of 1994, Indians fans were wildly excited about the prospects of finally having a winning team in Cleveland. They had the perfect mixture of free-agent veterans and young players in their prime. It

The last remnants of Cleveland Municipal Stadium. *Photo by Dr. Gosky.*

was a plan set in motion by high-profile general manager John Hart several years earlier. Hart talks about his good relationship with Indians owner Dick Jacobs and manager Mike Hargrove:

> *When you look at any sporting venue—and especially baseball—it comes down to the owner, general manager and manager being connected. As the manager, Mike Hargrove was very much included in everything we did all the way up to the ownership level. The thing I wanted to do as a general manager was to make sure that it was a locked-in group. I had Mike sit in on financial meetings so he could see what the club was facing economically. We would also bring in Dick and Mike to talk about the state of the team so that there was a blending of the people who knew. The worst thing that can happen in an organization is a lack of communication. We had a good connection because Mike was a field guy who was pretty secure in his own skin. He was the perfect manager for this young club and a good player's guy. There were never any real issues because we all knew our roles. I could walk into Mike's office and talk about what was going on on the field, and he could sit in an owner's meeting.*

Hart had several special roles in the Cleveland Indians organization, including a stint as team manager after Doc Edwards was fired. At one point, he ascended to the role of director of baseball operations. In 1991, Hart replaced Hank Peters as general manager and was named executive vice-president of the team. John Hart relates the transition from the field to the front office for the Cleveland Indians:

*I saw generations of fans that were so hungry for a winner because they hadn't had one. They had been through so many bad years, and they were fans that were loyal and connected with their players. I felt the excitement of being part of a turnaround. I also understood the baggage that the Indians had been carrying with them. I thought it was a tremendous opportunity and also realized that this was an original American League franchise. There was a rich history of baseball in Cleveland, and it gave me the "why not us" approach. We had been struggling through some low-win seasons, and when I came in, we had the chance to strip it bare and make as many good trades as we could. We wanted to have a development and scouting system in place to strip it and rebuild it. The last piece of this was getting Jacobs Field. I think it gave us the ability to add the pieces to the puzzle.*

Mike Hargrove was a former professional ballplayer who had spent time as a Cleveland Indian. He had a good career that spanned several seasons with Texas, San Diego and Cleveland. He was named American League Rookie of the Year in 1974 after he hit an incredible .323, the first Texas Ranger to ever receive that honor.

In 1985, Hargrove ended his playing career as a Cleveland Indian. Years later, his career path would bring him back to Cleveland, but this time he would be in the dugout. Midway through the 1991 season, he replaced John McNamara as the head coach of the Indians. Mike Hargrove discloses why he chose Cleveland as the best place to begin his career as a big league manager: "I knew Dan O'Brien and Joe Kline well from my days playing back in Texas. I felt as though my best chance to get back to the big leagues, either as a coach or manager, was with the Indians because they had all suggested that I should continue in a managerial position when I got done playing baseball. It was a comfort thing as much as anything."

Heading into the 1994 season, everyone around baseball realized that Cleveland was on the upswing, and it would be up to Hargrove to guide the team that Hart had masterfully put together. The amazing off-season trades and dealings between 1993 and 1994 cemented Hart's reputation as a genius. John Hart discloses some of the selling points that he used to bring free agents to Cleveland:

*For the first time, we had a core of players who were really good, and people around baseball were aware of how good they were. There was an opportunity in Cleveland that we should be considered among the elite because we had a very talented team. Those guys we brought in still had gas in the tank and understood how to win. I think the new stadium and the energy and excitement around Cleveland helped. People around the league were starting to talk about the energy that we were starting to build. That was the first year we ever made any of those phone calls to try and bring in veteran talent to go with our core group of young talent. We didn't even attempt to do it in prior years. We were met with a very positive reception from a lot of those guys, whereas just a year or two before, it was a "don't bother" sort of a deal.*

Following the 1993 season, Hart pulled the trigger on a deal that would singlehandedly change the course of Indians baseball for years to come when he traded Reggie Jefferson and Felix Fermin to Seattle for Omar Vizquel. Vizquel became one of the greatest shortstops to ever play the game. Vizquel had won his first Gold Glove playing shortstop with Seattle; he would win eleven more before his playing career ended in 2012. He also completed the perfect one-two punch with Kenny Lofton in the lineup. A great bunter, Omar had no problem getting Lofton over to third base after he had reached base and stolen second. His excellent play in the field also brought out the best in second baseman Carlos Baerga. The Indians had unknowingly struck gold.

Baerga shared what he liked most about playing with Omar Vizquel in the middle infield: "It was awesome! He was the best shortstop I have ever played with in my life. He was the guy who taught me how to play defense and prepare myself for a game. He made me work to become a good player. On his first day on the team, I agreed to teach him how to hit, and he agreed to help me become a better fielder. He was a very complete player who could bunt and hit and play great defense. He concentrated so hard on defense that every day we went to the field, he made me take at least thirty ground balls at live speed and turn the double play as if it were a real hitter. He taught me so many good habits on how to prepare for a game."

When Hart wasn't trading for Gold Glove infielders, he was signing future Hall of Famers such as Eddie Murray. The signing of a living legend like

Murray meant that the Indians were on the verge of bigger and better things. Adding Murray gave Cleveland the credibility it needed as well as a team leader both on and off the field. It was Murray who found a comfortable spot behind Albert Belle in the lineup, providing Belle with the protection he needed. He would be the team's designated hitter and also serve as first baseman when regular first baseman Paul Sorrento needed a day's rest.

The Murray pickup was big, but Hart was not done dealing as he managed to bring in veteran ace pitcher Dennis Martinez. El Presidente is considered one of the top Latin pitchers of all time. He was the first Nicaraguan to ever reach the Major Leagues. He was also on the 1983 World Series champion Baltimore Orioles team with Murray. He played for the Orioles from 1976 to 1986 and was a perennial ace in their rotation, leading the league in wins in 1981. In 1991, while pitching for the Montreal Expos, he managed to throw only the thirteenth perfect game in Major League history. He went on to lead the league in both ERA and shutouts that same season. Martinez was well respected by his peers, and the nickname "El Presidente" stuck with him wherever he played. He won one hundred games in Montreal before leaving the Expos after the 1993 season.

The addition of Dennis Martinez on December 2, 1993, was just the spark the Indians needed to collaborate with proven starter Charles Nagy. A couple months later, Hart added free agent Jack Morris. The once-questionable rotation was now very formidable with the likes of Nagy, Martinez, Morris and Mark Clark. The changes to the starting rotation allowed Nagy to drop back in the rotation and relieve him of considerable pressure. Nagy went on to excel in his new role as a middle-of-the-rotation starter.

Charles Nagy discusses his enthusiasm about playing in the new ballpark with so many great additions: "It was great! The Browns were struggling and about to leave town, so we were the best ticket in town. It was kind of a resurgence for us. I was excited to move into a new facility—even the groundbreaking ceremony was a lot of fun. A bunch of us had just signed long-term contracts, and we were excited for what lay ahead. We had great pieces added to the puzzle in the off-season. No one really knew what was going to happen in the future, but we knew we had a good team and good crop of guys."

Jim Thome also expresses his excitement about playing in the new venue: "The vibe and the energy was electric. When we moved into Jacobs Field, you could tell people were just so excited, and we fed off of that energy."

The key free-agent pickups helped better shape a team of young potential All Stars who were ready to hit their stride. The clubhouse leader and fan favorite was catcher Sandy Alomar Jr. Born into a family of baseball stars, Sandy's brother Roberto was a Gold Glove second baseman with the Toronto Blue Jays. Father Sandy Sr. grew proud watching both of his sons reach the Major Leagues and follow in his footsteps. Sandy Alomar Jr. came to Cleveland after the 1989 season in a trade that sent him, Carlos Baerga and Chris James to San Diego in return for All Star outfielder Joe Carter. At the time, it was a controversial trade because Carter was a fan favorite in Cleveland. But Clevelanders accepted the move since Alomar was a highly touted two-time minor-league player of the year. Alomar didn't disappoint, and he quickly rewarded the Cleveland management's faith in him by winning the 1990 American League Rookie of the Year Award.

The Indians and John Hart pulled off another steal when they traded for Lofton prior to the 1992 season. They sent backup catcher Eddie Taubensee and pitcher Willie Blair to the Astros. Lofton was yet another young prospect who Cleveland obtained with the hopes of becoming a decent player. What they got instead was a perennial All Star. Lofton wasted little time in 1992 showing the Indians brass that their confidence in him was warranted, hitting .285 and swiping sixty-six bases. The sixty-six stolen bases broke the American League rookie record; it was also enough to break the franchise record previously set by Miguel Dilone.

In 1993, Lofton continued to excel as he stole seventy more bases, leading not only the team but also the league. He was hitting for average as well as stealing the opposition blind every time he reached base. He quickly became a five-tool player, regularly taking extra-base hits and even home runs away while patrolling the Cleveland Municipal Stadium outfield. His leaping ability combined with his speed helped him become a Golden Glove winner in 1993. The award would be the first of four he would earn during his career. With Golden Glove winners Alomar behind the plate, Lofton in center field and Vizquel at shortstop, the Indians were rock solid defensively up the middle.

Kenny Lofton discusses what it was like coming to Cleveland and being a key part of the rebuilding project John Hart had in place:

> *I had played on a last-place team in Houston, so coming to Cleveland to join another team with a poor record wasn't much different at the time. It was more of an opportunity for me to play and show people what I could do. We had a lot of core guys, and you could tell that we were trying to rebuild into a winner. You could tell we were starting to get a lot of the pieces together. It was kind of tough playing in the old ballpark because we never had a lot of fans come to the games. You could tell the team and fans*

*were both looking for a winner. The fans were passionate and loyal despite*
*the constant losing. It was just a time when you knew the team needed to*
*start putting a winner on the field. In '92, it was very tough, but you could*
*tell that we were getting better and trying to do everything we could to win.*

Carlos Baerga was another key addition acquired in the Joe Carter trade with San Diego. In 1985, the Padres had drafted Baerga out of high school when he was only sixteen years old. In his initial season with the Cleveland Indians, Baerga played regularly at third base and did well. He hit for a .260 batting average and showed some power at the plate. Baerga continued to improve, and he solidified his position in the starting lineup as the full-time starting second baseman in 1991. That year, his average rose to .288, and he knocked in twenty home runs. The next year was a banner one for Baerga, as he amassed two hundred hits and finished the season with a .312 batting average. The fans fell in love with him because of his trademark smile and hustle. They remained behind him through some of the team's roughest times.

In the final week of the 1993 season, Baerga again managed to reach the 200-hit mark. In the hospital for an infection, he had to beg John Hart to check him out. After getting his 200th hit, he promptly checked back into the hospital when the game ended. That showed the passion Baerga had for his craft and also his dedication to teammates and fans. He had accomplished a rare feat with the back-to-back 200-hit seasons, becoming the first second baseman to do it since Roger Hornsby in 1922. Baerga made the All Star team in both the 1992 and 1993 seasons. The Indians were starting to amass plenty of young talent with Baerga, Alomar and Lofton, all of whom reached their peak at the same time.

Carlos remembers his early years in Cleveland fondly:

*When I was traded here as a nineteen-year-old from the San Diego Padres,*
*I never thought I would have the career with the Indians that I did. Thanks*
*to God that my first manager, John McNamara, made me feel so good and*
*taught me how to prepare myself and be a professional both on and off the*
*field. It really helped me out to have someone who had confidence in me.*
*The Indians gave me the opportunity to be here in the big leagues, and that*
*doesn't happen too often. I had the opportunity to come off the bench, and I*
*prepared myself for that. Then they gave me the chance to play second base,*
*and it was something special. We still had fans coming to the ballpark in*
*the beginning when we were really bad. Even though the team was bad, I*
*loved hitting in the old ballpark because I felt I hit better there. Then we*

*came to Jacobs Field, and the fans loved it first and then the players loved it next. I remember the first game against Randy Johnson and having the ballpark packed. It truly was something special.*

Carlos had the following to say about the addition of key free agents who led to higher expectations for the Indians' 1994 season:

*John Hart made the young players feel happy by giving them multi-year contracts. It gave us the chance to play and improve without worrying about the numbers; it took the pressure off of us. I was the first one to sign, followed by Kenny Lofton and Albert Belle. It was a commitment to the players, and that allowed us to step up. It allowed us to have fun and put everything together to win games and do well. Then he brought in all the good free agents to further help us win. It was a winning recipe because we were so close when the strike set in. We were only one game back, so I knew we were going to the playoffs. We had the confidence we had been building from spring training on, and we didn't want to lose it.*

While Lofton and Baerga had been setting the table, it was power-hitting left fielder Albert Belle who was reaping the benefits of knocking them all in. Belle had struggled with some serious personal problems early in his career while playing under his middle name, Joey. He needed to get his life and career in order because he was to play a key role in the Indians rebuilding project. Pitchers feared his intimidating presence and physical stature. When Belle overcame his personal problems, he became unstoppable. He had an intense glare that would strike fear into even the most seasoned veterans who dared to face him. His power numbers increased yearly as he became one of the most feared hitters in baseball. He hit twenty-eight home runs in 1991, thirty-four in 1992 and a career-high thirty-eight in 1993 (to go along with 129 RBIs). Belle was just another weapon in the Indians' growing offensive arsenal.

John Hart had done an amazing job assembling talent for Mike Hargrove to manage. The 1994 roster was a work of beauty that had come together with a little luck and plenty of skill. With the key factors in place, it left a small crack in the door just wide enough for two young hungry lions to come charging through it.

Mark Lewis had been the established third baseman, but few fans believed he would hold onto the job for much longer with the powerful, young Jim Thome nipping at his heels. Thome was a throwback player; he ran laps before the game on the outfield grass and wore his socks up high. He pointed his bat to center field before every pitch just like Roy Hobbes did in the movie *The Natural*. His work ethic was unmatched, and it was only a matter of time before he overtook Mark Lewis for the full-time starting spot at third.

The final piece of the rebuilding puzzle was rookie right fielder Manny Ramirez. The twenty-two-year-old superstar was bursting with talent when the Indians saw him playing at George Washington High School in New York City. Selected as the thirteenth overall pick in the 1991 MLB draft, Ramirez tore through the minor leagues in little time, emerging as one of the top prospects in baseball. In 1993, he was named the Minor League Player of the Year by *Baseball America*. His minor-league numbers were astronomical at the time of his call-up—he was hitting .333 with thirty-one home runs and 115 RBIs between Double A and Triple A. Those statistics were almost identical to those of the eventual American League MVP, Frank Thomas.

Kenny Lofton discusses some of his first impressions of playing at Jacobs Field and the drastic improvement of the team:

> It started off with some great free agents like Eddie Murray, Dennis Martinez and the trade for Omar Vizquel. We had Felix Fermin, but they wanted a younger shortstop, so we got Omar. Veterans like Dennis Martinez and Eddie Murray helped complete a great mixed core of older guys and younger guys. It was one of those things where you wanted to see how it would work out when combined with the excitement of playing in a new ballpark. Everything was starting to come into place because everyone was looking for a winner in Cleveland. We had a strong second half in 1993; our record improved and showed how strong our main core of players were. We did so well that people were very excited to see what we had going forward—that was the big thing heading into the 1994 season. We had a young core group of talented players who were driven to win, and we were able to pick up a few free-agent pieces to the puzzle, which kept everyone excited.

Everything was in place to open the new ballpark, Jacob's Field, with a championship-contending team. They had the Golden Gloves with Lofton, Vizquel and Alomar combined with the veteran leadership of Murray, Martinez, Morris and Nagy. The young guns—Ramirez and Thome—blended together with the core of Belle and Baerga. This cornucopia of talent was under the direction of a sharp baseball mind in Mike Hargrove. It would take each player working with his teammates to reach the highest level. Hargrove describes what it was like to have so much talent coupled with the excitement of moving into a beautiful new ballpark:

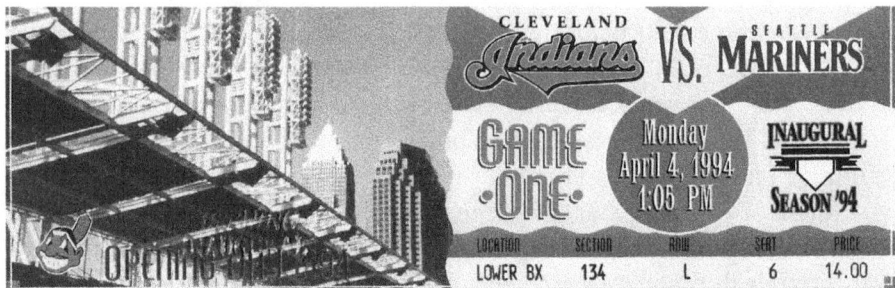

Opening Day 1994, the first at Jacobs Field. *Photo by Nicole Ponyicky.*

*It is hard to put into words the depth of the excitement anytime you have a passion for what you do and the stars start aligning toward the thing you've been building for. It made us real nervous but also very excited. The unknown was a little daunting, but it was a great time. We started this thing out with the core players: Baerga, Belle, Alomar, Lofton, Whitten, Clark, Nagy, Plunk and guys like that. We had a mixture of veteran players in 1992 and 1993 who really taught our young kids how to win. Then we heard from a number of people around the league that they really liked our ball club and that we had a good thing going. It was a perfect storm with the new ballpark. I really feel that if a player has talent and feels good about who he's working with and who he's working for, the talent really has a chance to take off. Our players enjoyed playing for John Hart and myself, and we had a good coaching staff. The brand-new ballpark was the ace of baseball at the time—it just amped everything up even more.*

The Cleveland Indians opened up the Jacobs Field era with the first regular-season game on April 4, 1994. The ceremonial first pitch was thrown out by President Bill Clinton in front of a sold-out crowd of 41,459 excited fans. The excitement in the air was so thick it could be cut with a knife. The pitching matchup that day was Dennis Martinez versus lanky left-hander Randy Johnson of the Seattle Mariners. The Mariners were managed by Lou Piniella, widely considered one of the best in the game. They had the league's most intimidating pitcher in Johnson, as well as its best young hitter, Ken Griffey Jr. The Mariners were a very formidable foe against which to open the new ballpark.

After getting leadoff hitter Rich Amaral to ground out to Baerga to start the game, Martinez hit Edgar Martinez with a pitch. From there, Martinez issued back-to-back walks to Ken Griffey Jr. and Jay Buhner, which loaded the bases without allowing a single hit. Eric Anthony hit a sacrifice fly deep enough for Edgar Martinez to tag and score, giving Seattle the early lead. Tino Martinez flew out to Manny Ramirez in right field to end the inning.

Randy Johnson suffered from some of the same Opening Day nerves as he walked two of the first three batters he faced. He worked his way out of the first-inning jam by not giving up any runs or hits. Despite his early wildness, the tall lefty seemed to have his best stuff, and it looked like it could be a long afternoon for the home team.

Dennis Martinez meets with Tony Peña on the mound. *Photo by Dr. Gosky.*

After a scoreless second inning, Seattle got back on the scoreboard with an Eric Allen solo home run, the first official hit of the game and of the stadium. It was a costly one for Martinez, who already had walked several batters but had managed to pitch his way out of trouble until the home run. To make matters worse, it seemed the Mariners' two-run lead was almost insurmountable, as Johnson was keeping the Indians scoreless and hitless.

When Johnson took the mound to start the bottom of the eighth inning, the Indians had yet to earn a single hit. The fans and players were wondering if the worst would actually happen. When Alomar singled through the hole between short and third, everyone shared in a collective sigh of relief. Candy Maldonado had walked before Alomar, and suddenly the Indians had two on with no out and their first legitimate scoring threat of the game. A few moments later, Johnson threw a wild pitch that allowed both men to advance.

Ramirez hammered the next pitch into deep left field for a two-run double to tie the game. In a matter of a few moments, the Indians went from being hitless to tying the game. It wasn't long after that when Ramirez exposed one of the few flaws in his game by getting picked off second base. It ended the momentum, but not before the Indians evened the score and showed the magic that Jacobs Field would become known for.

*Left*: Eddie Murray was a key pickup heading into the 1994 season. *Photo by Dr. Gosky*.

*Below*: Omar Vizquel and Kenny Lofton made for a great one-two punch at the top of the lineup. *Photo by Dr. Gosky*.

*Opposite*: The trade for Omar Vizquel was the biggest move of John Hart's career. *Photo by Dr. Gosky*.

The ninth inning proved to be uneventful as both teams failed to score. It was evident that this new ballpark was destined to provide exciting finishes as game one went into extra innings, only increasing the drama.

José Mesa took the hill to start the tenth inning and quickly gave up a hit to Griffey. Jay Buhner laid down a beautiful bunt to move Griffey into scoring position with only one out. Mike Hargrove decided to pull Mesa in favor of Derek Lilliquist. The move looked like it was the right decision when Lilliquist forced Eric Anthony to pop out to first base. Tino Martinez drew a walk that forced Lilliquist to face Kevin Mitchell with two on and two out. Mitchell singled, which allowed Griffey to score and give Seattle the lead 3–2. Hargrove went back to his bullpen, and Eric Plunk managed to get the final out.

Bobby Ayala pitched the bottom half of the frame by striking out Alomar. Ramirez drew a one-out walk, and Piniella decided to replace Ayala with Kevin King. Jim Thome replaced Mark Lewis and doubled to right field, advancing Wayne Kirby, who was pinch-running for Ramirez, to third base. The Indians now had two men in scoring position with just one out, giving them an excellent chance to win it. Piniella took advantage of the open base and walked Lofton to load them up and create a force-out at any base. Vizquel ruined Piniella's plans when he sacrificed a ground ball out to score Kirby from third and once again tie the game. Carlos Baerga followed with a fly out to center field to end the inning, but not before the Indians had managed to tie the game 3–3.

Eric Plunk had no problem mowing down the bottom half of the Seattle order and keeping the game tied into the bottom of the eleventh inning.

In the bottom of the eleventh, King forced Belle to ground out to first before Eddie Murray came up and crushed a double. One batter later, Paul Sorrento sacrificed Murray over to the third base and put the winning run a mere ninety feet away. It was high drama after the intentional walk to Alomar brought Kirby to the plate with a chance to win it. Kirby had been the Indians starting right fielder for several years before Hargrove and Hart chose to give his position to the rookie sensation, Ramirez. The Jacobs Field crowd roared as Kirby singled a soft line drive into shallow left field to score Murray from third base and earn the Indians their first win in their beautiful new home.

The Indians used the memorable Opening Day victory as momentum to propel them to a hot start, winning six out of their first seven games. They finished April with a 13-9 record and appeared to be getting better each week. They got red hot in June by winning ten games in a row. They had an impressive 51-33 record by the All Star break, a record good enough to put them in a first-place tie in the newly formed American League Central Division.

On August 10, the Cleveland Indians beat the Toronto Blue Jays 5–3 in front of more than fifty thousand fans at the Toronto SkyDome. The win gave them an impressive 66-47 record, only one game out of first place. But Cleveland fans' worst fear occurred the following day when MLB players went on strike. The work stoppage was not resolved during the regular season, and it ended up causing the rest of the season to be canceled. The baseball strike was a nightmare to all of Cleveland because for the first time in years, they had a great baseball team. But it had come to a premature end through no fault of their own. Mike Hargrove explains what the baseball strike meant for the team: "It was tough, and we knew it was coming. In reality, the last time we had an in-season strike was in the 1981 season. And when that happened and it was over, they declared first- and second-half winners, so we were hoping that may happen again if it was a short strike. I wanted us to finish ahead of the White Sox, so we really played and managed for that two-week period leading up to August 12 like it was the last game of the season. We were trying to make a big push to catch the White Sox, and we almost did it."

The Indians had been on a roll since that dramatic Opening Day victory, and they never looked back. Four of their five starting pitchers had at least ten wins. Dennis Martinez was 11-6, while Jack Morris held a record of 10-6. Charles Nagy was 10-8, Mark Clark was rolling with a 10-3 record and three of the starters had an ERA under 4.00.

The pitching wasn't the only thing going well—the hitting was the best it had been in franchise history. Eight of the players had double-digit home runs, including Albert Belle, who led the team with thirty-six. Belle was also batting .357 with 101 RBIs—strong numbers that would have contended for, if not won, the batting title and MVP award if a full season would have been played. Lofton was batting a career-high .349 with sixty stolen bases at the time of the work stoppage. Both young power hitters, Thome and Ramirez were living up to their hype as well with twenty and seventeen home runs, respectively. At .254, Eddie Murray, who was one of the veteran hitters brought in to guide the lineup and clubhouse, didn't have the best batting average, but his seventeen home runs and 76 RBIs were exactly what the Indians needed from him.

Kenny Lofton discusses the pain of the great season ending prematurely: "We were on such a roll that it was disappointing to see the strike. A lot of guys like myself and Albert put up a lot of great numbers for the season. It was a time when the team and city realized that we were an upcoming young team ready to win, and the strike cut it short. But we knew 1995 was going to be a big year for us."

Charlie Nagy shares his pain caused by the strike: "We all came together in 1994 and had a great start. We were playing great baseball when the strike happened. The most disappointing thing for everyone was how the whole thing carried on because we thought it would last only a week. The playoffs were looming as we were right in the thick of the race, and all of a sudden, everything just came to a grinding halt. We had to set our sights on 1995." Jim Thome adds, "We felt like we were just getting going at that time. It was frustrating because we worked so hard to have the strike cut us short. We were very disappointed."

The Indians had everything a great team needed. The only thing that could stop them was what they couldn't control. It was a terrible way to end a great season. It wasn't just the fans who were upset with the strike. John Hart also shares his disappointment: "We felt we had a team that was World Series bound when we traded for Dave Winfield during the strike—and then Bud Selig announced we weren't going to play anymore baseball. It was a very painful time." Fans could only hope that if and when play resumed, the Indians could somehow match what they had done that season. Little did anyone know that the following year would go down as one of the most memorable and best in baseball history.

Chapter 2

# TRIBE FEVER

On April 2, 1995, baseball fans across North America breathed a sigh of relief when the 232-day Major League Baseball strike finally ended. The player strike had eliminated the previous year's World Series and cast a dark shadow over baseball. When the strike ended, it meant not only that baseball would start anew in 1995 but also that the Cleveland Indians would have a chance to prove that their 1994 season wasn't a fluke.

John Hart wasted no time improving the Indians by signing Orel Hershiser. This off-season addition strengthened the already impressive starting rotation. Hershiser was well respected throughout the league and was considered the missing link that would take Cleveland to the playoffs.

John Hart saw something in Hershiser and felt that the rewards far outweighed the risk. With Martinez and Nagy already in place, coupled with the later season addition of Ken Hill, the Indians rotation became one of the most talented and experienced in baseball.

By the time the season began on April 27, 1995, the Indians were more than ready to pick up where they had left off the previous season. They began the 1995 season with an 11–6 win in Texas against the Rangers. As they approached a critical series on Memorial Day with the Chicago White Sox, they were rolling along with a record of 18-9. The White Sox were seen as the division favorite by many experts, and it was predicted that it would only be a matter of time before they caught up with the Indians for the Central Division lead. The Indians knew that a sweep of the White Sox would quiet the critics and show that they were a real threat to win the

The free-agent signing of Orel Hershiser was another major coup pulled off by John Hart.
*Photo by Dr. Gosky.*

division. That is exactly what they did as they took all four games from the White Sox and never looked back.

At the All Star break, the red-hot Indians had accrued a 46-21 record with a staggering twelve-game lead in the division. They were well represented at the Midsummer Classic All Star Game at Coors Field, home of the Colorado Rockies. Carlos Baerga was starting at second base, and Albert Belle was voted in as the starting left fielder. Sitting in the bullpen were Dennis Martinez and José Mesa. Having four Cleveland Indians on the All Star roster was something almost unheard of just a few years prior. This was another sign that the Cleveland Indians were becoming one of the elite teams in baseball.

On Friday night, September 8, 1995, in the words of Tom Hamilton, "a season of dreams became a reality" when the Indians beat the Baltimore Orioles in front of a sold-out crowd at Jacobs Field to clinch the Central Division. It was their first playoff berth since 1954 and ended a drought that eclipsed most fans' entire lives. It was a moment that many fans believed they would never see and one that defined a generation of die-hard fans.

When the season ended, the Indians had won the division by an astronomical 30 games over the second-place Kansas City Royals. They finished the year on a five-game winning streak that brought their final record to 100-44. They were the only team in American League history to win 100 games in a season that was shorter than 154 games.

The 1995 season became known by many as a season of dreams as the Indians dominated the American League. Mike Hargrove, the manager of this talented team, reflects on the positives and the challenges of coaching the extremely talented roster:

> *The 1995 season was shortened because of the strike, and we ended up winning 100 out of the 144 games, which is really hard to do. The season was unique because I don't think we ever lost more than 3 games in a row. We had a tremendous offensive ballclub, so it was a magical season. Normally during a season, you will have your ups and downs with major fires to put out, but that year there weren't huge fires to put out. We had a new hero every night, so that made it a real fun season. The challenge was to keep the players focused the entire season. We had such a large lead, so the biggest challenge was keeping everyone focused on what we wanted to accomplish—that was more than just getting to post season but also winning a world championship. I had a lot of help with a great coaching staff and veteran leaders. The veteran players really did a nice job policing the clubhouse. They were guys who had been there before and were able to teach our young kids how to win.*

Carlos Baerga also recalls the magical 1995 season:

> *Everyone followed our team like we were the Yankees. We would beat anyone, and our confidence was so high. We won 100 times in only 144 games, and not too many people can do that. It was an unbelievable lineup, and we were living a dream. We were so cocky and felt like we couldn't be beat. Before our first playoff game against Roger Clemens, we were yelling at him from the dugout, saying, "We are going to kill you tonight—you better be ready!" It was really a special time. I couldn't believe I got to hit third in that lineup for six years. At least six players from that lineup should go into the Hall of Fame. It was a very special lineup, and I got to hit third. It didn't matter the pitcher or the inning—we knew we could score. The Indians fans should be very proud of that team. I was very lucky to play with players of their caliber and players who cared about the game the way they did. We would work out every winter.*

*Left*: Albert Belle crushed fifty doubles and fifty home runs in a strike-shortened 1995 season. *Photo by Dr. Gosky*.

*Below*: José Mesa was lights out in any save situation during his 1995 streak. *Photo by Dr. Gosky*.

Charles Nagy reflects on what made his 1995 season one of his best: "We had a phenomenal team with a lot of great comebacks—that was one great thing about having such a talented lineup. As long as you pitch your innings and give your team a chance to win…it was just incredible. As pitchers, we just went out there and tried to give our team a chance to win every night. We knew if we just stayed out there long enough, that was going to happen. We just had a great group of guys."

Kenny Lofton adds:

*We had a job to do, and everyone knew his role. As individual players, we knew exactly what we needed to do to win. We each had our roles and did our best to perform them. I knew I had to get on base so Omar could get me over. From there, Carlos, Albert, Eddie and Sandy had the job of getting me in. We all knew what we had to do because we did our job. I don't think people understand just how important that is. It takes a group of players to focus on doing their part for a team to be successful. In 1995, we pretty much did that. We understood our exact roles, and I knew that if I did my job of getting on base, my teammates would know exactly what their jobs were as well. It was just magical during the season with Mesa closing the games and all those comebacks we had. We didn't have the best pitching staff, but they were good enough to give us the chance to score enough runs to win, and we did exactly that.*

The excitement of the fans was at an all-time high as the playoffs began with the Indians set to do battle with the AL East winners, the Boston Red Sox. Tribe fever had the fans in a frenzy during that time, and Indian T-shirts, sweatshirts and jerseys were being sold everywhere.

Game 1 of the Division Series took place on October 3, 1995, in front of an enthusiastic crowd at Jacobs Field. Not even the long rain delay before the game could damper the spirit of the fans. On the mound for Cleveland was veteran Dennis Martinez. His opposing pitcher was one of the greatest to ever play the game, Roger Clemens. It was the kind of matchup that baseball purists were excited to watch.

Boston scored first in the third inning on a two-run home run by John Valentin. Dennis Martinez had been pitching very well up to that point. The early lead seemed much bigger than just two runs, as Roger Clemens was shutting down the powerful Indians lineup, holding them scoreless through five innings. Perhaps the damp weather was keeping the hot bats at bay. Whatever the issue, it was urgent that the Indians get on the board before it became too late.

The Indians' bats started to heat up in the bottom of the sixth inning. Omar Vizquel started the two-out rally when he drew a walk. Carlos Baerga followed with a single, which gave the Indians men on the corners with two outs. When Albert Belle hit a two-out two-run double to tie the game, Jacob's Field became unglued. It was a mammoth double for Belle that set the stage for Eddie Murray to knock him in with a single, putting the Indians ahead 3–2. It was up to the Indians' bullpen to hold onto the lead. They did that until the top of the eighth inning, when Boston managed to rally and tie the game. Multiple rain delays mixed with a couple lead changes meant that this game was headed for a possible all-night affair.

The game remained tied past the midnight hour as it entered the eleventh inning. If the Indians were to earn their first playoff win in forty-seven years, they would have to battle from behind again. Tim Naehring hit a Jim Poole pitch over the wall in left field to give the Red Sox a 4–3 lead. Poole managed to get out of the inning without giving up any more runs, but the damage had been done.

Bob Costas was calling the game and said, "The last time Belle faced Aguilera, he homered." It was as if the moment was destined to happen. The words had just left Bob Costas mouth only seconds before Albert Belle smashed a fastball from Rick Aguilera over the wall to tie the game. Seconds after Albert Belle rounded the bases, Boston manager Kevin Kennedy stormed the field to protest. He demanded that Belle's bat be confiscated and taken in for inspection. It was his claim that Belle had been corking his bat and that the home run was not legitimate. A few moments later, Cleveland manager Mike Hargrove stormed the field to argue with the umpire, who allowed the bat to be taken away. Hargrove explains what was going through his mind at that moment: "I have a real quick and bad temper; I get angry quick, but I can also get over things quickly. That was one of those times that it was a real good thing that I was that far away from the dugout. If I were much closer, I would have been in there. I thought it was a real bush-league move—they knew that Albert wasn't using a corked bat. It was gamesmanship trying to avert Albert's attention. It was just a chickenshit move, to tell you the truth, and I wanted to make sure Kevin knew that." The crowd was going nuts as Belle shot a look into the Red Sox dugout and pointed to his bicep. It was a heated moment that showed the fight and heart of the team.

Later in the inning, Tony Peña came to the plate with two outs and two on base with a chance to win the game, but he grounded out to second base. It was a golden chance for Peña to play the hero, but he failed to capitalize

*Left*: Tony Peña hit one of the most memorable home runs of all time to win Game 1 of the 1995 ALDS. *Photo by Dr. Gosky*.

*Below*: Catcher Sandy Alomar Jr. *Photo by Dr. Gosky*.

on it. It wouldn't be much longer until he received another chance at glory, this time cashing in.

Just over five hours after the first pitch had been thrown, with most of northeast Ohio fast asleep, Tony Peña hit a thirteenth-inning two-out solo home run off of veteran pitcher Zane Smith to deep left field that gave the Cleveland Indians their first playoff win in nearly half a century. The image of seldom-used backup catcher Tony Peña running around the bases with both arms up in the air in victory is one that will live in the memories of Cleveland fans forever.

Orel Hershiser tossed a Game 2 gem as the Indians rolled past the Red Sox 4–0 to take a two-game lead in the series. Boston countered with Erik Hanson, who pitched well himself, but a two-run double by Omar Vizquel in the fifth proved to be too much for Boston to overcome. A two-run home run in the eighth by Eddie Murray was added insurance. It was a dominant win that gave the Indians full momentum as they headed into Boston for Game 3.

For Game 3, Tim Wakefield was the last line of defense for the Red Sox as they hoped to avoid the sweep. The Fenway crowd was taken out of the game early when Jim Thome hit a two-out two-run home run, giving Cleveland the early lead. The bottom continued to fall out for Boston in the next inning as Jim Thome again did the damage by drawing a bases-loaded walk to give Cleveland a 3–0 lead. The Red Sox managed to score in the fourth and draw back to within two runs before the Indians put the game out of reach with a five-run sixth inning. Paul Sorrento hit an RBI single that was followed by an RBI double from Sandy Alomar Jr. Omar Vizquel joined the hit parade with a two-run single followed by an RBI double from Carlos Baerga. It gave Cleveland an 8–1 lead, which would be enough to close out Boston and move on to the American League Championship Series against the Seattle Mariners.

It seemed as though the stars were lining up for the Indians. They looked to get an early jump on Seattle as they had swept Boston and were able to rest as the Mariners fought in a five-game battle with the New York Yankees. The series took every ounce out of Seattle's starting rotation, including having to use their ace, Randy Johnson, in extra-innings relief to close out Game 5, making him unavailable in the first two games of the series with the Indians. Former Cleveland Indians general manager John Hart remembers that post-season well: "We sat on the tarmac for an hour and a half waiting to find out if we were going to New York or Seattle as their Game 5 was ending. We didn't want to go to Seattle at first because we would have had to face Randy Johnson. Then in the ninth inning of that game, the Mariners

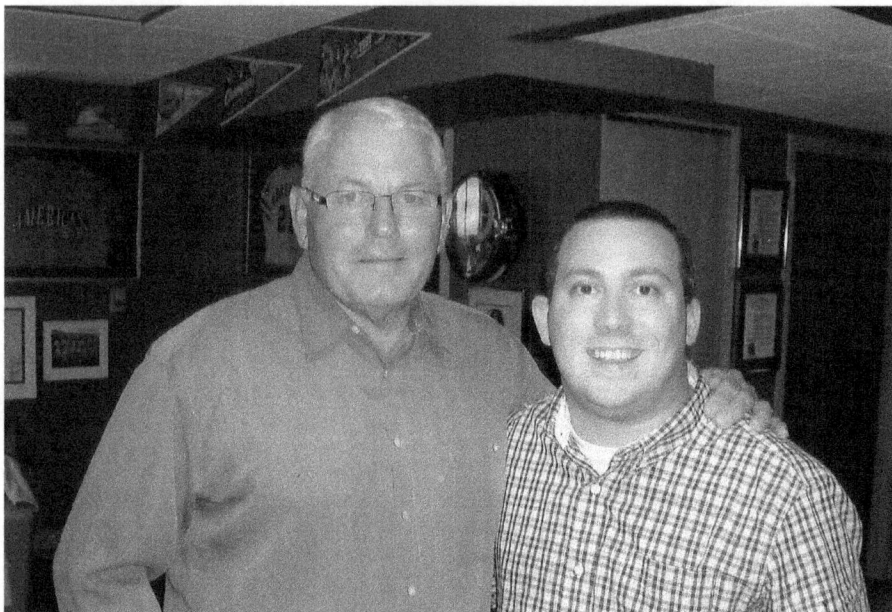

Mike Hargrove, pictured here to the left of the author, was chosen to lead this talented bunch. *Photo by Vince McKee.*

The Indians celebrating another win on their way to the World Series. *Photo by Dr. Gosky.*

had to bring in Randy Johnson in relief, so we started rooting for them. Then they won, and we were happy because we found out that we would face unknown Robby Walcott. I said, 'Get the reports out because we are going to light this kid up!'"

Despite the fact that they had to open on the road, the Indians remained confident as they prepared to face unknown pitcher Bob Wolcott. Cleveland loaded the bases in the first inning on three straight walks. With Albert Belle coming to the plate, it looked as though Game 1 was on the verge of a possible blowout before even one out had been made. Then, Wolcott shocked everyone by promptly striking out Belle, forcing Eddie Murray to pop out and getting Jim Thome out on a hard hit ball, allowing him to get out of the inning unharmed.

The failure of the Indians to score proved costly in the bottom of the second when Mike Blowers put Seattle on the scoreboard with a two-run homer. Dennis Martinez was pitching well but left the pitch up, and Blowers took it out of the ballpark. Jim Thome was able to knock in an RBI single in the top of the third, putting the Indians back in the game. Albert Belle hit a solo home run off of Wolcott in the top of the seventh inning, and just like that, the game was tied. The tie would not last for very long, however, as Jay Buhner hit a one-out double to start a Seattle rally in the bottom of the seventh. Two batters later, Luis Soho hit another double off of Dennis Martinez, giving Seattle a 3–2 lead that it would hold onto for the win.

Game 2 was a pitching matchup between veteran pitchers Orel Hershiser and Tim Belcher. The game was a pitchers' duel until the top of the fifth, when Carlos Baerga broke the scoreless tie with a two-run single. In the top of the sixth, Manny Ramirez's solo home run and Sandy Alomar Jr.'s RBI triple increased the Indians lead to 4–0. Ken Griffey Jr. hit a solo home run in the bottom half of the sixth to get Seattle on the board. Manny Ramirez hit his second home run of the game in the top of the eighth, increasing the Indians' lead to 5–1. The Mariners managed to score again in the ninth, but it was too little too late as the Indians won 5–2.

Game 3 brought American League Cy Young winner Randy Johnson to face Cleveland at Jacobs Field. Seattle quickly provided the giant pitcher with a two-run lead by scoring off of Charles Nagy in both the second and third innings. Cleveland was able to rally for a run in the bottom half of the fourth when Kenny Lofton, who continued to be a thorn in Johnson's side, led off with a triple. Moments later, Omar Vizquel sacrificed Lofton in with a long fly ball that cut the lead in half. The score remained 2–1 until the bottom half of the eighth, when Kenny Lofton singled and drove in pinch runner Wayne Kirby to tie the game. Kenny Lofton was wreaking havoc on the normally unflappable Randy Johnson.

Cleveland Indians manager Mike Hargrove called on his strong bullpen as the game entered extra innings. Seattle caught the bullpen off guard and managed to tag them for three runs in the top half of the eleventh when Eric Plunk gave up a three-run home run to Jay Buhner. The blow was too devastating to overcome as the Mariners held on for the 5–2 victory, retaking the lead in the series.

It was a devastating but character-building loss for the Indians, who came out stronger the next night for Game 4. If the Indians were to climb back in the series, they would have to do it shorthanded as both Albert Belle and Sandy Alomar Jr. were out of the lineup with injuries. The Mariners were sending Andy Benes to the mound against the Indians' Ken Hill.

The Indians wasted no time jumping on Benes in the bottom half of the first inning as Carlos Baerga hit a sacrifice groundout that put them ahead 1–0. Eddie Murray, who was batting cleanup because of the injury to Belle, followed with a two-run home run that put Cleveland up 3–0. One inning later, Lofton hit a sacrifice fly to increase the lead to 4–0. The next inning, Jim Thome hit another two-run home run to increase the lead to 6–0 and ended all doubt as to the outcome of the game.

Ken Hill was mowing down Seattle hitters one by one, and it looked apparent that the series would soon be even. In the seventh inning, Omar Vizquel hit an RBI double that increased the lead to 7–0. The Mariners were not able to score a single run, and Ken Hill picked up his first playoff win as a Cleveland Indian.

With the series tied at two games apiece, it was time for the pivotal Game 5 at Jacobs Field. Mike Hargrove decided to skip Dennis Martinez's scheduled start in favor of the hot hand of Orel Hershiser. It was a gutsy move but one that Hargrove was confident would work based on Hershiser's excellent playoff history. Going for the Mariners in Game 5 was veteran pitcher Chris Bosio. The game had all the makings of a baseball classic, and did not disappoint.

The Indians jumped on Bosio in the first when Vizquel reached on an error. Carlos Baerga followed with a single, giving the Indians two on with only one out. Albert Belle struck out, which made the Eddie Murray at-bat even more dramatic. Murray came through with a two-out RBI single that put Cleveland ahead 1–0.

Orel Hershiser managed to hang on to the lead until the top of the third, when Ken Griffey Jr. hit an RBI ground-rule double to tie the game. Seattle scored again in the fifth to take the lead 2–1 after an ill-timed error. With the pressure mounting, Jim Thome stepped up in the bottom of the sixth and smashed a two-run home run deep into the right-field stands of Jacobs Field to give the Indians a 3–2 lead. The home run knocked Chris Bosio from the game.

In the top of the seventh, the Mariners had the top of their order coming up to face the Indians bullpen. Relief pitcher Julian Tavarez managed to get one out, but not before getting himself into a bit of trouble and allowing two runners to reach base. Hargrove wasted no time pulling Julian Tavarez in favor of his left-handed specialist, Paul Assenmacher, to face the two best hitters in the Seattle lineup. Assenmacher showed he was up for the test as he set down both Griffey Jr. and Buhner with beautiful back-to-back strikeouts. He made two of the best hitters in baseball look clueless with an excellent display of off-speed breaking balls. A few innings later, José Mesa closed the game out in the ninth, and the Cleveland Indians were only one win away from going to the World Series.

Cleveland traveled back to Seattle for Game Six in the raucous Seattle Kingdome. The date was October 17, 1995, and the Cleveland Indians were only nine innings away from returning to the World Series for the first time since 1954. Standing in their way was a six-foot-ten giant nicknamed "The Big Unit." Randy Johnson was the most feared pitcher in all of baseball and an eventual five-time Cy Young Award winner. He appeared in ten All Star Games before his playing days were over and was known for having a wicked slider and untouchable fastball. And he excelled against left-handed hitters.

Taking the mound for the Indians was veteran ace Dennis Martinez, who had a lot to prove after being bumped from his regular start in Game Five. Seattle had a refuse-to-lose attitude for months as they overcame a large deficit in the Western Division, behind Anaheim, to capture the division in a sudden-death playoff game. They were used to having their backs against the wall and played their best when they were in a must-win situation. It would be the job of the crafty veteran right-hander Martinez to shut them down for good and punch the Indian's ticket to the World Series.

How did the Indians get ready for this critical Game 6? Mike Hargrove recalls what he told the team in the clubhouse before the game: "You don't have to tell guys in that situation too much because they are fully aware of the magnitude of the situation. They knew what was going on, so we didn't have to prepare them for too much. We had played top pitchers well all year long, so I wasn't really worried about us not being able to get to Randy. I was more worried about shutting down their great offensive ballclub." Carlos Baerga remembers the pre-game strategy on how the team decided to beat Randy

Johnson: We had a meeting before the game and decided we needed to score runs by bunting the ball and making them crazy. We wanted to get him pissed off at us. We had to force him to make mistakes and not wait for the big home run. The little things would be important for us to win. We told Kenny to steal bases and bunt on him because we needed to get Johnson crazy. It was so loud that night that we needed to put in earplugs—that on top of having to face a giant on the mound. It was crucial to win that game because it was going to be tough to have to come back and face them for Game 7 if we didn't. It turned out to be one of my biggest games as I went three for three against him and hit a home run. It is something I will never forget."

The Indians were clinging to a 1–0 lead as they entered the top half of the eighth inning. Tony Peña continued his post-season heroics by leading off with a double to deep right field. Pinch runner Ruben Amaro was then inserted in the game to replace Peña on the base paths. Kenny Lofton continued to play mind games with Johnson as he bunted to the right of the mound, where Johnson was unable to field the ball in time to throw him out. The Indians now had runners on first and third with no outs. Lofton continued to wreak havoc as he stole second base, which put two men in scoring position with no outs. Johnson, who was clearly rattled from Lofton's antics on the base paths and his ability to get big hits off him all series long, threw the next pitch wild and past catcher Dan Wilson. As Amaro strolled home on the wild pitch, Johnson slowly walked to home plate with little to no urgency, unaware that Lofton was flying past third base and heading for home. By the time Johnson realized what was going on, it was too late as Lofton flew past him to score the second run of the play. It was a backbreaking moment for Johnson and Seattle as the heart and hustle of Lofton had given Cleveland a 3–0 lead late in the game.

Kenny explains why he had so much success against Randy Johnson:

*My goal was to help the team…Cleveland hadn't been in the playoffs in a long time. It was my job to do the best I could, and I was a guy who always looked for a challenge. The challenge presented itself with the best pitcher in the league, and I wanted it. I wanted to go against him and do whatever I had to do to take care of my job as the leadoff hitter. I wanted to be the guy out there to see how good he was because it was a challenge for me. I think in the 1995 playoffs, it was a challenge, and I felt like I was the best leadoff hitter in the game facing the best pitcher in the game. My job as a leadoff hitter was to rattle him up and get the team going. I felt comfortable as a leadoff guy, and it didn't matter who was on the mound because I just*

*wanted to go out there and do my job to help my team. My teammates told
me that when I went, they went. I needed to do my job as a leadoff hitter
for the rest of the team to be able to play well, and it worked out. We ended
up doing some magical things.*

Lofton goes on to explain the magical play few fans will ever forget:

*You always have to be aggressive—I always made sure to run the bases hard.
You should always turn each base corner with the intent for something to
happen. In that situation, by me naturally doing what I do on a passed ball,
it naturally dictated for me to do what I did. On that play, as I rounded third,
I looked at the player and the ball and just kept my speed going. I looked up in
front of me and didn't hesitate to keep going. I just felt like being aggressive; I
just needed to react. It was more of a reaction thing than anything else. I just
saw the play in front of me and reacted. As a guy with speed, you have to go
off your instincts and reactions, and that's what I did.*

Omar Vizquel took the next Randy Johnson pitch to deep left field before
it was tracked down just in front of the warning track for the first out. It
would be the last out recorded by Johnson as the next batter, Carlos Baerga,
smacked a solo home run over the wall and put Cleveland ahead 4–0,
chasing Johnson from the game in the process.

Julian Tavarez showed his relief pitching dominance by shutting down all
three Mariners batters he faced in the bottom of the eighth. The Cleveland
Indians were only three outs away.

Cleveland fans everywhere held their breath as José Mesa took the mound
in the bottom half of the ninth inning. For more years than anyone would care
to remember, the Indians had been the joke of baseball. There had even been
movies, like *Major League*, that poked fun at the long losing history our city had
endured. José Mesa was only three outs away from ending all the jokes and
putting Cleveland back on the sports world map once again.

Mesa began the bottom of the ninth by forcing Ken Griffey Jr. to ground
out to Carlos Baerga for the first out. Edgar Martinez, who was having a stellar
series, struck out and brought the Indians just one out away from the World
Series. But the Indians would have to wait a little longer, as Mesa walked Tino
Martinez to extend the drama one more batter. Jay Buhner then swung at a
0-1 fastball from Mesa and hit it on the ground to Jim Thome at third base.
Thome fielded the ball cleanly and threw it across the diamond to first base to
record the final out and send Cleveland fans into a frenzy.

*Left*: In 1995, the World Series returned to Cleveland for the first time in forty-one years. *Photo by Bob Lamb.*

*Below*: A shot of the scoreboard from Game 5 of the 1995 World Series versus the Atlanta Braves. *Photo by Bob Lamb.*

Mike Hargrove shares his feelings as the Indians brought the pennant home to Cleveland: "I will never forget when Jim Thome caught that ball to win the division earlier in the season. I don't think that it really struck me that we were actually going to the World Series until I had showered and was walking to the buses. It was a real sobering and exhilarating moment and also pretty cool!" General manager John Hart also remembers the celebration in Seattle fondly:

> *Carlos Baerga and my wife danced down the hallway in Seattle after the series win. It was a great night with Dennis Martinez beating Randy Johnson and winning the American League pennant. When we won the pennant that night, it was one of the best-pitched ballgames I have ever seen. Martinez was fabulous and slowed the game down doing what he did. I remember going down to the locker room and seeing all the guys we traded for and young players who came up together. It was a great group. Then I looked over and saw all the veterans like Orel, Eddie, Dennis and Tony Peña. I looked at this group of guys that were finally going to a World Series in Cleveland, and I sat over in the corner and cried like a baby. We really were going to the World Series, and it was a very special time.*

The World Series saw two great pitching performances by Greg Maddux and Tom Glavine in Games 1 and 2 in Atlanta to give the Braves a 2-0 lead heading back to Jacobs Field. The Indians managed to take Games 3 and 5 wrapped around a Game 4 loss to force the series back to Atlanta. Game 6 saw the Braves win by a narrow 1-0 margin and take the World Series. It was a somber end to an amazing season.

Charlie Nagy, who won Game 3 for the Indians, discusses his emotions about pitching in the first World Series game in Cleveland in forty-one years: "It was just awesome being in Cleveland at that time and seeing the whole renaissance of the city. The energy that the fans brought day in and day out propelled a lot of our wins that season and led us into the playoffs. We were excited to put Cleveland back on the map and show off the city and its great fans. With the way the city embraced the fans, it was just great to be a part of it."

Kenny Lofton explains why the Indians struggled in the 1995 World Series against Atlanta:

> *We had an incredible season, leading the American League in almost every single offensive category. We had the best team, and we knew the proper strike zone. I feel that the strike zone in the World Series was not correct. It*

*was not the way we were used to seeing it called. If the ball is over the plate, it is a strike, and if it is off the plate, it is a ball. We had to go out of our element and swing at balls off the plate because the umpires were calling it five inches off the plate for the Atlanta Braves. The umpires were giving the Atlanta Braves pitchers a wide strike zone. We were used to swinging at balls on the plate and not off the plate. It took us off our game because that's not who we were. It took us off our game as a team because we were used to getting all the walks and doing what we were supposed to do to get on base. For me it was tough as a leadoff hitter to try and swing at a ball off the plate because that's not what I was taught to do. I was taught that if the ball is off the plate, you don't swing. In the World Series, it got us all messed up, especially in the National League ballpark. They were not calling the strike zone accurately. That is the biggest reason—we had to go outside of our element to play the game of baseball.*

Jim Thome disagrees with Lofton when asked about the series, stating, "They threw strikes and pinpointed their pitches very well. They knew how to change speeds. They had greats like Maddux, Glavine, Smoltz and Avery. They knew how to pitch to our lineup, something not many teams knew how to do. We had a very talented lineup, and you have to give the Braves a lot of credit because they pitched great."

Two years later, with a revamped roster, the Cleveland Indians returned to the Fall Classic. It would go down as one of the most exciting World Series of all time. Cleveland fans everywhere wondered if this time the last game would end in victory.

Chapter 3

# TWO MORE OUTS

The expectations were high heading into the 1996 season for the Cleveland Indians. They had made it to the World Series the prior season for the first time in forty-one years, losing to the highly talented Atlanta Braves in six closely contested games.

They had nearly the entire starting lineup coming back with the exception of first baseman Paul Sorrento, who had gone to Seattle. Sorrento was replaced by a returning Indian from years earlier, Julio Franco. It was a fairly lateral move as Sorrento's and Franco's 1996 numbers were close, with Sorrento having the slight edge in power.

While the majority of the roster continued with their dominant ways, Eddie Murray and Carlos Baerga seemed to be struggling. In a surprising move, John Hart dealt Eddie Murray to the Baltimore Orioles halfway through the season. In return for Murray, the Indians received pitcher Kent Mercker. It was a surprising move, but nothing compared to what Hart was set to do just eight days later.

On July 29, 1996, John Hart made a trade that broke the hearts of many, if not all, Cleveland Indians fans. He sent fan favorites Carlos Baerga and Alvaro Espinoza to the New York Mets in exchange for shortstop José Vizcaino and second baseman Jeff Kent. It sent shockwaves throughout Cleveland. Carlos Baerga was struggling badly, but not many fans expected the sudden trade. In the summer of 2013, during his introduction into the Indians Hall of Fame, John Hart reflected on the trade: "It was the hardest trade I ever had to make. Carlos was a defining player in an earlier trade and was one of the first guys we bought into Cleveland when we wanted to do multiyear contracts. He was such a large part of the team and such a leader. He was the happiest player in our locker room and was great. His first five years in the big leagues drew comparisons to Roger Hornsby. I loved my players, but I had to take that hat off and make moves for the best of the organization. It was painful because of the relationship that I had with Carlos and still do to this day."

Carlos Baerga was a core player in the organization for many years, and the news shocked him as well as his many legions of fans. Carlos had the following to say when asked about how hard it was to be traded:

> *In the beginning, it was very hard because I didn't understand why I was being traded. We had a very good record and were headed to the playoffs again. I was hurt in the playoffs the year before when I had hurt my ankle. I was never healthy, and the decision was hard to take because I was happy here and the captain of the team. It was something that took me a couple years to forget about. I understand it better now. I had lost my concentration for the game and preparation for the game. Things happen for a reason in life, and I'm more mature now and able to talk to my son about it. I explained to him what happened to me and also tell a lot of young players to be careful. When you put on a uniform, you represent an entire organization, so you have to be cautious of what you do off the field. Sometimes you may lose your job because you lose that focus.*

The Indians went on to win the Central Division again in 1996 but never seemed to recapture the magic of 1995. With poor pitching and the newcomers never quite fitting in, the Indians were upset in the first round of the playoffs by the upstart Baltimore Orioles. It was an early end to the season, and the Indians organization would have to face numerous off-season questions.

On October 28, 1996, power-hitting left fielder Albert Belle became a free agent. Most fans assumed that it would only be a matter of time before Belle resigned with the Indians. In the first of many signs to come that baseball is still a business to many players, Belle betrayed his hometown fans and signed with the rival Chicago White Sox. He joined perennial All Star Frank Thomas, and with the new power duo in place, many in the media declared the White Sox as the new team to beat.

With Albert Belle gone, the Indians needed to replace his power in the lineup and searched for a trade to do so. John Hart found his trade partner

David Justice and Matt Williams were two key additions heading into the 1997 season. *Photo by Dr. Gosky.*

with the San Francisco Giants, who were looking to improve their defense. On November 13, 1996, Hart sent José Vizcaino, Julian Tavarez and Jeff Kent to the Giants for power-hitting veteran third baseman Matt Williams. Williams made the National League All Star team in 1990, 1994, 1995 and 1996. He led the majors in home runs in 1994 by hitting forty-three in only 112 games during a strike-shortened season. Many felt that if the season had gone the full length, he could have broken the home run record of sixty-one, set by Roger Maris. His power matched that of teammate Barry Bonds, and the duo became one of the most feared combinations in all of baseball. Along with his power, Williams also brought three Gold Gloves Awards with him. His fielding had been good enough to win the award in 1991, 1993 and 1994.

Williams's signing forced third baseman Jim Thome to learn a new position: first base. Thome's power numbers were too good to remove him from the everyday lineup, and he was young enough to learn a new position. Thome again proved how much of a team player he was by welcoming the

*Above*: Mike Hargrove checks on new leadoff hitter Marquis Grissom. *Photo by Dr. Gosky*.

*Left*: Matt Williams smashed several home runs in the 1997 regular season. *Photo by Dr. Gosky*.

new challenge. Thome had this to say about the transition to first base: "I had just become comfortable at third base and had to take on this unknown. With losing Albert, we needed Matt Williams. It was ironic that year because I ended up making the All Star team, which is great karma when you think about it."

The biggest move took place just a week before the new season was set to begin. On March 25, 1997, John Hart once again shocked Indians fans when he traded away perennial All Star and fan favorite Kenny Lofton, along with reliever Alan Embree, to the Atlanta Braves. In return, the Braves sent power-hitting outfielder David Justice and speedy leadoff hitter Marquis Grissom. Kenny Lofton recalls being shocked by the trade:

> *I was called into the office from the clubhouse, and I didn't think too much of it. Then I saw Davie Nelson with a strange look on his face, and I started to wonder what was going on. They told me I was traded. I asked why, and they said that they were worried I was going to leave in free agency after the season was over. I asked them why they didn't bother talking to me about this first, and they said they just expected me to demand the same amount of money Albert did and that they couldn't afford it. It was basically a done deal, and I was pretty shocked. I didn't know what to do. I was heartbroken, but it was out of my control. I just felt like if they had talked to me in the beginning about this whole thing, it never would have happened. But they didn't, and that is what happened. It was a shock, but I had to live my life. I was disappointed, but I had to move on.*

The addition of Justice was met with a mild reception by the Cleveland fans, as the memory of him hitting the winning home run for the Braves in the 1995 World Series was still fresh in their minds. Despite the sour memories, he was a talented player who would combine with Williams, Thome and Ramirez to create a potent lineup.

Mike Hargrove shares how he handled all of the player changes while molding the team into a contender: "Players of that caliber make it somewhat easier. It wasn't like we traded away Kenny Lofton and brought in Joe Blow. We thought Grissom and Justice were dynamite players in their own right. We knew it was coming because we had talked about a possible trade earlier in spring training, so when it did happen, I wasn't surprised. It was one of those things that you learn to live with. In baseball, the more things stay the same, the more they change. I felt like that, with the ballclub we had and the hitters we brought back, we would be alright."

Matt Williams stretches out after a well-deserved single. *Photo by Dr. Gosky.*

Sandy Alomar crosses home plate after hitting the winning home run in the 1997 All Star Game at Jacobs field. *Photo by Dr. Gosky.*

Sandy Alomar was named All Star Game MVP at his home ballpark. *Photo by Dr. Gosky.*

At the All Star break, the Indians had reached a season-high eight games over .500 at 44-36. They were catching fire at the right time and looked to have a strong second half. The Midsummer Classic that year would be held at Jacobs Field. It was a spotlight for Cleveland as "The Jake" was widely considered one of the nicest ballparks in baseball. The excitement over having the All Star Game in Cleveland gave the city an extra reason to puff out its chest.

The Indians' hottest player was Sandy Alomar Jr., who was in the midst of a thirty-game hitting streak and was on pace to surpass all of his career-high numbers. He added to his great season with an outstanding performance in the All Star Game. The ballgame was tied 1–1 when Sandy came to the plate with one on in the bottom of the seventh inning. If there were any doubts that Sandy was having a special season, they were quickly erased when he hit a Shawn Estes fastball over the fence to give the American League a 3–1 lead. The AL team would hold on to win, and Alomar was later named the game's MVP.

The Indians rode the wave of momentum from the All Star Game to win five out of seven following the break. They stayed consistent the rest of the way and finished the season in first place with a record of 86-75. It wasn't the usual dominant season, but it was enough to get them back into the playoffs. One of the biggest question marks of the 1997 season was the role of closer.

The 1997 season was different from years past in that the Indians won the division but hadn't dominated the league. The season record was the lowest of all division winners heading into the post-season. Hargrove recalls that the team felt like the underdogs heading into the playoffs: "I felt that no one was picking us to do anything. We had always played well when we had to in years past; the tougher the competition, the tougher we played. There were a lot of rough spots on the road that season, and we didn't find our identity until late in the season at Anaheim. It was Jim Thome's birthday, and all the players got together and decided that they would pull their socks up high to honor him. We won handily, so we decided to do it again and got on a roll. That was the rallying point of that season, and it brought that team together. They jelled after that and became good."

Game 1 of the division series in New York ended badly for the Tribe. They had gotten off to an early five-run lead, but the bullpen struggled, and they lost by a score of 8–6.

Game 2, in Yankee Stadium in the Bronx, took on a desperate feel for the Indians. Down 1-0 in the series, they knew they couldn't afford to lose. They turned to their rookie sensation, Jaret Wright, who quickly made everyone question the decision to start him by walking the bases loaded in the bottom of the first. The Yankees would make him pay with a two-run double by Tino Martinez, followed by an RBI sacrifice fly by Charlie Hayes. Before the fans in Yankee Stadium could digest their first hot dogs, the hometown team had spotted starting pitcher Andy Pettitte a three-run lead.

But the Indians knew from their own experience in Game 1 that no lead is safe when playing October baseball. Jaret Wright settled down and mowed down Yankee hitters in order for the next few innings. The Indians still trailed 3–0 when they went up to bat in the top half of the fourth inning, but something in the air was about to change drastically. After Pettitte forced Bip Roberts to line out to center field to begin the inning, he allowed a single to Vizquel, who then advanced to second on a throwing error. Pettitte rebounded by striking out Manny Ramirez but then walked Matt Williams. With two on and two out, David Justice hit a single that gave Cleveland its first run. Sandy Alomar Jr. and Jim Thome followed with singles of their own, tying the game at 3–3. Tony Fernandez followed suit and hit a two-run double that put Cleveland ahead by a score of 5–3. One inning later, Matt Williams hit a two-run home run and increased the Cleveland lead to 7–3.

While the Cleveland bats were coming alive, Jaret Wright was silencing the Yankee bats. After a shaky first inning, he rebounded to throw five scoreless innings, striking out five and allowing only two more hits. Wright showed incredible mental toughness and assured manager Mike Hargrove that he would be ready if called on again. José Mesa took the mound a little earlier than normal when he came on in relief with one out in the eighth inning. The Yankees proceeded to make things interesting by scoring on Mesa in the eighth and then again in the ninth on a Derek Jeter home run. But Mesa and the Indians managed to hold on for the 7–5 victory to even the series. Mike Hargrove explains how important the come-from-behind win was to the team: "We lost a lot of Game 1s, but the one thing is that a team feeds on a history. I'm talking about the history of the team dating back to the 1920s. All the players on the ballclub realized the Indians as a whole were really a pretty good ballclub. I think that what we had done in the recent history of 1995 helped keep our focus and realize that it was just one game."

The series moved to Cleveland for Game 3, and noted Indians killer David Wells took the mound for the Yankees. It was a quiet Saturday night for Indians fans as the Yankees used a four-run fourth inning to take a 6–1 lead and never looked back. David Wells was dominant, and Charles Nagy couldn't get out of the fourth inning. It wasn't looking good for Cleveland.

Game 4 shaped up to be a battle of two veteran playoff heroes from the 1980s: Orel Hershiser and Dwight Gooden. The Yankees jumped on Hershiser in the first by scoring two runs with clutch hits by Derek Jeter and Paul O'Neill, who continued to have an amazing series. The Indians cut the lead in half with a solo home run by David Justice in the second inning. Both pitchers then settled down, and the score remained 2–1 heading into the bottom of the eighth. The Indians were down to their last six outs and facing Mariano Rivera, one of the greatest closers of all time. Rivera wasted no time in striking out David Justice and forcing Matt Williams to fly out. He was only four outs away from eliminating Cleveland from the playoffs, but he had to face a man who was having a season of destiny. Sandy Alomar Jr. stepped up to the plate, and it was almost as if no other hitter in all of baseball was more qualified for that moment than him. Sandy continued his dream season by crushing a Rivera fastball over the right-field fence to tie the game.

Mike Jackson took the mound in the ninth and set down the Yankee lineup in order. It was up to Ramiro Mendoza to try to hold down the Indians hitters and send the game into extra innings. Marquis Grissom led off with a single. Bip Roberts sacrificed Grissom over to second with a bunt, which brought Omar Vizquel to the plate with a chance to win it. Omar wasted no time hitting a single off Mendoza. The ball had enough steam on it to roll past Derek Jeter and into shallow center field, allowing the speedy Grissom to score from second base and win the game.

It was high drama heading into Game 5 as, once again, manager Mike Hargrove rolled the dice and started Jaret Wright. It was a gutsy move to start a rookie in such a high-profile game, but Hargrove had faith in Wright after watching him shut down the Yankees in Game 2. Hargrove looks back at his decision: "Jaret was the hardest thrower we had on the ballclub. He didn't have a lot of pitches, but he pitched well in New York in a tough spot. I just felt that he was a tremendous competitor—I'm not saying that someone else wasn't, but he just had a knack to really bear down and focus, which gave him that pinpoint concentration to be as good as he should be and even a little bit better in those situations." Wright proved Hargrove's faith well founded as he pitched four consecutive scoreless innings to start the game. Meanwhile, the Indians were doing well against Yankee starting pitcher Andy Pettitte. They used singles by Grissom and Roberts to set the table for a two-run double by Manny Ramirez. Matt Williams followed the Ramirez double with an RBI single, giving the Indians a 3–0 lead. One inning later, in the fourth, Tony Fernandez hit a sacrifice fly that stretched the Indians lead to 4–0.

The Yankees slowly climbed their way back into the game, managing to score three runs and cut the lead to 4–3 heading into the ninth. Cleveland Indians fans took a deep breath as José Mesa took the mound in the top of the ninth. He forced Tim Raines and the red-hot Derek Jeter to ground out to get two quick outs. But Paul O'Neill continued to be a thorn in the Indians' side by hitting a two-out double and keeping the game alive. Bernie Williams then smashed a Mesa fastball to deep left-center that looked like it may leave the park before landing softly in Brian Giles's glove and sending the Indians back to the American League Championship Series.

Up next for the Tribe would be the American League Eastern Division champion Baltimore Orioles. This was a perfect chance to get revenge on the team that had beaten them the previous year in the playoffs. It would be a tall task as Baltimore was loaded with veteran talent and excellent pitching. The series would begin in Baltimore as the Orioles had the better regular-season record.

Game 1 proved to be a pitchers' duel as Baltimore starting pitcher Scott Erickson threw a four-hit shutout. Chad Ogea did a good job as well, giving up only three runs, but it was three too many as Baltimore took a one-game lead in the series.

Cleveland ace Charles Nagy took the mound for Game 2 hoping to even up the series. The Indians gave him the early run support he would need by scoring two off of Baltimore veteran starter Jimmy Key in the first inning. Manny Ramirez's two-run home run gave Nagy the early lead. The Cleveland lead would not last long, however, as Cal Ripken Jr. hit his own two-run home run to tie the game. The game would remain tied in a tight pitchers' duel until the bottom of the sixth, when Mike Bordick hit a two-run single off of Nagy, giving Baltimore the 4–2 lead and knocking Nagy from the game. The Cleveland bullpen, composed of Alvin Moorman, Jeff Juden, Paul Assenmacher and Mike Jackson, held the Orioles scoreless and kept the score at 4–2 heading into the eighth.

The Orioles' Armando Benitez, one of the best relief men in baseball, took the mound in the top of the eighth inning. This would have spelled doom for most teams. However, the Indians were not most teams and had actually had good success against Benitez in the past. The table was set for high drama, and Benitez would not disappoint. Benitez managed to strike out two of the first four batters he faced to start the inning. The problem for him was that the other two drew walks and brought Marquis Grissom, the go-ahead run, to the plate. Benitez continued to have horrible luck against Indian batters as Grissom crushed his pitch over the wall for a three-run go-ahead home run. Suddenly, after two games of futile hitting, the Indians held a 5–4 lead and were only six outs away from evening up the series before heading back home for Game 3. Jackson and Mesa got the six outs, and the series was tied.

Jacobs Field was packed on a sunny Saturday afternoon as fans watched one of the greatest pitched games in playoff baseball history. Orel Hershiser and Mike Mussina used the shadows of the setting sun against opposing batters all game, and the game remained scoreless through six and a half innings. The Indians finally broke through against Mussina in the bottom of the seventh inning, when Matt Williams singled to center field to score Jim Thome and give Cleveland a 1–0 lead. Mussina followed by getting two quick groundouts, and after seven innings, he and Hershiser had combined for a remarkable twenty-two strikeouts and only one earned run.

José Mesa took the mound in the top of the ninth with the Indians clinging to a 1–0 lead. He immediately gave up a leadoff single to Chris Hoiles. Two batters later, Brady Anderson hit a fly ball that Marquis Grissom somehow lost in the lights, allowing it to fall in for a double and the tying run to score. Just one game earlier, Grissom had been the hero, but now he was in position to be the goat.

The game remained tied 1–1 heading into the bottom of the twelfth when Randy Myers took the mound for Baltimore and struck out Brian Giles to start the inning. Marquis Grissom, who seemed to be in the middle of every crucial situation, came up to bat and managed to draw a walk. Tony Fernandez followed the Grissom walk with a single to right field, putting the winning run ninety feet away. With Grissom on third and only one out, Mike Hargrove called for Omar Vizquel to lay down a bunt in the hopes of sacrificing Grissom home to score. Omar attempted to lay down the bunt on the next pitch, but the ball missed his bat; however, it also missed catcher Lenny Webster's glove. The alert Grissom, who was already halfway down the line, came home to score uncontested. It was a highly controversial call, but it gave the Indians the win and a 2-1 lead in the series. Baltimore manager Davey Johnson and catcher Lenny Webster argued soundly, but it was too little too late. One of the finest pitched games in playoff history had ended on a fluke play and given the Tribe the win.

A pivotal Game 4 took place in Cleveland with young Jaret Wright on the mound. Despite getting some early run support from a two-run Sandy Alomar Jr. home run, Wright struggled to remain consistent and fell behind 5–2 after only three innings. Geneva, Ohio native Brian Anderson was called on by Hargrove to keep the game close. Cleveland would attempt to mount a comeback against Baltimore pitcher Scott Erickson, who had previously shut them down in Game 1. Manny Ramirez hit a solo home run with one out in the bottom of the fifth to bring the Indians to within a couple runs. Jim Thome and David Justice followed with back-to-back singles. After a Matt Williams strike out, Sandy Alomar Jr. hit an RBI single to score Thome. Baltimore relief pitcher Arthur Rhodes then walked Giles before throwing a wild pitch that allowed Justice to score from third and tie the game. As Justice scored, Webster lost track of the ball after colliding with the umpire. In the middle of the confusion, Alomar was able to race home and score to take the lead. It was another wild play in a series that had been filled with them.

The Indians had a 7–5 lead to hold onto for the second half of the game. Their bullpen looked sharp, giving up only one run and handing José Mesa a 7–6 lead to start the ninth. Mesa, who had blown the save the prior day, again looked shaky as he took the mound. He walked Roberto Alomar to start the inning and then gave up a single to Geronimo Berroa that allowed Roberto to advance to third base. Mesa recovered to strike out Eric Davis before giving up the game-tying single to Raphael Palmeiro. Mesa had blown two saves in two days; it was a bad omen of what was to come a few weeks later.

Mesa was able to get out of the inning without giving up any more runs, and the game remained tied 7–7. Manny Ramirez led off the bottom of the ninth inning with a walk and was sacrifice-bunted over to second by pinch hitter Kevin Seitzer. Veteran pitcher and former Cleveland Indian Jesse Orosco forced David Justice to fly out for the second out before Davey Johnson pulled him for Armando Benitez. With first base open, Benitez gave Williams the free pass and decided to pitch to Sandy Alomar Jr. With the previous record Benitez had against Cleveland combined with the magical season Alomar was having, it came as no surprise when Alomar hit the game-wining single to score Ramirez.

The Indians brought a commanding 3-1 series lead into Game 5 with the hopes of clinching the series in front of their home crowd. Baltimore pitchers Scott Kamieniecki and Jimmy Key put a stop to any celebration plans the Indians may have had with a shutout through eight innings. Chad Ogea had no offensive support for his second straight start, and the Indians ended up losing 4–2. It was a critical loss because it meant that the series would return to Camden Yards in Baltimore for Game 6.

Game 6 took place on Wednesday, October 15, 1997, on a sunny afternoon in Baltimore. The fans in attendance and watching at home viewed a classic as, for the second straight start, Mike Mussina was untouchable. Luckily for Cleveland, so was their ace, Charles Nagy. Through ten innings, the game remained scoreless, and Cleveland had managed only two hits. With the Indians preparing to bat in the top of the eleventh, Baltimore reliever Armando Benitez jogged in from the bullpen. Benitez was looking to shake off his past playoff-game demons against Cleveland, and he put away the first two Indians hitters with ease.

In a storybook finish that was right out of a Hollywood script, Tony Fernandez hit a Benitez fastball over the wall in left field to give the Indians the lead. That was all they needed as José Mesa closed it out in the ninth and sent Cleveland back to the World Series. Mike Hargrove explains what happened in batting practice before the game that led to Tony Fernandez getting the start over Bip Roberts and the eventual series-clinching home run: "I always felt that when you get in those situations where you indicate to whatever degree you can't go, its best we don't have you on the field. Bip came to me and said that he had flu-like symptoms, and I told him that he wasn't playing. I know it pissed him off, but if you don't want out of the game then don't tell me you're sick. All you're doing is saying that you don't have a lot of confidence in your ability to do your job and looking for an excuse. In those situations, we don't need people like that around." Roberts not wanting to play in those games was a surprise even to Hargrove, who recalls, "Yeah, I was shocked!"

The World Series returned to Jacobs Field in October 1997. *Photo by David Murphy.*

Chad Ogea played great in the 1997 playoffs. *Photo by Dr. Gosky.*

Hargrove shares other memories from that playoff series: "There were three big things that stick out. The first was the Vizquel suicide squeeze when Lenny Webster lost his mind and the game. The second was when we ran the wheel play earlier in the game to get us out of a jam. The last thing was the Tony Fernandez home run to win the series in game six." He goes on to reveal how the Indians dominated Armando Benitez during the series: "He was tipping his pitches, both his fastball and his split. If our veteran hitters had any idea what you were going to throw, they could hit it really hard. He would come set in his glove, and when his glove was straight up and down, it was a fastball. When it was laid over to the side, it was a splitter."

Charlie Nagy explains what led to his performance in Game 6: "We had a great defense behind us with a lot of new faces. It was a little bit different year, but we came together in spring training with a mission to win. I had great teammates who sacrificed and worked hard all season to put us in that position. I was lucky enough and fortunate to keep us in the ball game long enough to win."

The Florida Marlins were an expansion team that had come into the Major Leagues in 1993. Most fans outside of Miami didn't pay much attention to them because the Marlins rarely gave them any reason to. Just prior to the 1997 season, the Marlins loaded up their lineup with some high-priced free-agent talent to go along with a little bit of homegrown talent. For the first time in their short history, they became a viable threat in the National League. To the surprise of many, they made the playoffs and swept the San Francisco Giants in the first round before knocking off the defending National League champion Atlanta Braves to advance to the World Series.

Game 1 of the World Series took place on a hot Saturday night in Miami. Orel Hershiser had built a reputation as a post-season ace. It came as a surprise and a disappointment to Cleveland fans that Hershiser had his worst playoff outing that night, giving up seven runs in only five innings. The worst blows were back-to-back home runs from Moises Alou and Charles Johnson. The Indians battled back with solo home runs from Manny Ramirez and Jim Thome, but it was too little too late, and they dropped Game 1 7–4.

Being down one game was a familiar place for the Indians as they had lost both opening games in the previous two playoff series. Game 2 would be a greater challenge as they faced the Marlins' ace, Kevin Brown. Taking the hill for the Tribe was Chad Ogea, who had pitched well in the ALCS despite his 0-2 playoff record. Ogea allowed one run in the first inning and then nothing after that, looking sharp all night long. Timely hitting combined with a Sandy Alomar Jr. two-run home run gave Cleveland the 6–1 victory and sent the tied series back to Jacobs Field.

Frigid air greeted the teams as they arrived in Cleveland for Game 3. With the temperature just above freezing, it remains one of the coldest World Series games in history. The elements should have favored starting pitchers Charles Nagy and Al Leiter, but the results were anything but favorable for either of them.

Nagy allowed a first-inning solo home run to Gary Sheffield that would set the tone for the rest of the night. The Indians scored two runs in the bottom of the inning on back-to-back RBI singles by Matt Williams and Sandy Alomar Jr. to take a 2–1 lead. A bases-loaded walk to Gary Sheffield in the top of the third tied the game 2–2. In the top of the fourth, Darren Daulton hit another solo home run off Nagy, and Florida retook the lead. Florida handed Al Leiter a one-run lead as he took the mound for the bottom half of the fourth inning. Leiter wasted no time allowing Cleveland to tie the game by walking four of the first six batters he faced. Manny Ramirez followed the walks with a bases-loaded two-run single to put Cleveland ahead 5–3. The scoring was far from over, however; in the following inning, Jim Thome slammed a two-run home run to make it a 7–3 Cleveland lead.

Charles Nagy continued to struggle despite being given a four-run lead. The Marlins used a two-run home run by Jim Eisenreich to climb back into the game in the top half of the sixth. One inning later, timely hitting by Edgar Renteria and Gary Sheffield allowed Florida to tie the game. The Cleveland fans were freezing, but the Marlins' bats were on fire.

After a scoreless eighth inning, relief pitcher Eric Plunk took the mound to start the ninth in hopes of holding the Marlins' bats silent for another inning. Unfortunately, what unfolded was a series of Indians mistakes and blunders that led to a seven-run inning for Florida. It was walks, errors and wild pitches that spelled doom for the Tribe. The Indians managed to score four runs of their own in the bottom half of the ninth before losing the game 14–11. Mike Hargrove reflects on the loss: "Your job as a manager is to prepare for the worst and hope for the best. And sometimes no matter who you have playing, things just get out of your control. It was just one of those things. They won all the odd games, and we won all the even games, so it was back and forth. Both teams played really hard and really well, and it was a nail-biter all the way through."

The Indians had let one get away in Game 3, and they vowed to play sharper in Game 4 the following evening. Mike Hargrove once again turned to his rookie sensation, Jaret Wright, to try and even the series. Wright rewarded Hargrove's faith in him by tossing a scoreless first inning. A two-run home run by Manny Ramirez off Florida starting pitcher Tony Saunders

Jaret Wright meets with the media before Game 4 of the 1997 World Series. *Photo by Dr. Gosky.*

gave Cleveland a 2–0 lead. Later in the inning, Sandy Alomar Jr. hit an RBI double, and the Indians jumped out to a quick 3–0 lead. A couple innings later, RBI singles by Alomar Jr., Tony Fernandez and David Justice expanded the Cleveland lead to 6–0. Jaret Wright was cruising along and gave up only three runs through six innings. He received plenty of run support, including a two-run home run by Matt Williams in the eighth that finished the scoring with the Indians on top 10–3. It was a dominant win, and it evened the series heading into what would be a pivotal Game 5. Mike Hargrove explains the importance of providing Jaret Wright with an early lead in his first World Series start: "It is much easier to play ahead than it is from behind because you can be more aggressive. It's really important when you have a young kid on the mound because you beat the other team by putting more pressure on them than they do you. So anytime you can get a lead and put the pressure on the opposition, it gives you a chance to bury them."

Game 5 was a rematch of Orel Hershiser versus Livan Hernandez. The Marlins raced out to a quick 2–1 lead against Hershiser heading into the bottom of the third. The red-hot Sandy Alomar Jr. then turned the tide back in Cleveland's favor as he smashed a three-run home run to put them on top 4–2. Things stayed that way until the bottom fell out for Hershiser, who gave up a three-run home run to Moises Alou in the top half of the sixth. Later in the inning, Eric Plunk relieved Hershiser and promptly gave up a bases-loaded walk to increase the Florida lead to 6–4.

Hernandez held the Indians lineup in check through eight innings and did not allow them to score again. The Marlins scored two more insurance runs and held an 8–4 lead heading into the bottom of the ninth. José Mesa, who continued to look shaky, had given up one of those runs in the top of the ninth. The Indians fought hard and rallied for three runs in the bottom half of the ninth to draw within one run. Florida closer Rob Nen walked the tightrope as he gave up RBI singles to Jim Thome and David Justice but managed to hold on and secure the 8–7 win for the Marlins. The series was headed back to Florida, where the Marlins had two chances to win it all.

All the pressure in Game 6 was mounted squarely on the shoulders of Cleveland's starting pitcher, Chad Ogea. He was matched up against highly touted Marlin starter Kevin Brown. Some of the media did not give Ogea a chance of coming out the victor. But what the media and others didn't count on was the heart shown by Ogea, who went out and pitched a gem.

Ogea kept the Florida batters silent throughout most of the game, allowing just one run through five innings. Ogea was contributing not only on the mound but also at the plate, driving in the first two runs of the game with a two-run single in the top half of the second inning. Mike Hargrove shares why he thought Ogea was so effective in Game 6: "Chad was a good athlete and competitor despite not being able to throw the ball ninety-five miles per hour. He was more in the range of eighty-nine to ninety-one with a nasty change-up. Florida was a pretty good fastball-hitting ballclub, so it was his change-up and his competitive nature that helped him play so well. He also turned out to be our best hitter in the lineup that evening. It was just one of those things that played into his strengths."

Cleveland was holding on to a 4–1 lead heading into the bottom of the ninth, thanks to a pair of RBI sacrifice flies by Manny Ramirez. Despite giving up a triple, José Mesa was able to hold the Marlins scoreless, and the series became tied. A dramatic Game 7 was set for the following night.

Game 7 was set for Sunday, October 26, 1997, at Pro Player Stadium in Miami. Mike Hargrove hoped to celebrate his birthday with a World Series championship that evening. The fans of Cleveland wished for the end of a miserable forty-nine-year run without a World Series championship. Mike Hargrove shared what he told the team before the start of Game 7: "Again, there is nothing to say. You play so many games, and by then it was October 26, which was my birthday. So there is not a whole lot you can say that they are ready to listen to; they are ready to play. We had a short meeting before, as well as a pitchers' meeting and hitters' meeting, so they knew what they had to do. They knew it was Game 7." The hopes of everyone would rest on the shoulders of rookie Jaret Wright. Hargrove was not only skipping over Charles Nagy's spot in the rotation but also pitching Wright on short rest. Hargrove explains why he started Jaret Wright over Charles Nagy: "That was a tough decision. Charles Nagy was one of my all-time favorite players. I just felt like that every time we asked Jaret to pitch in a crucial game, he did a great job. I felt like it gave us our best chance to win." Hargrove personally told Nagy that he wasn't starting the game. He shared how difficult it was to make that choice: "It was really hard because of my own personal feelings for him and because he had been one of our best pitchers during the season. It was a very difficult decision, but despite not being too happy with it, Charlie understood and accepted it."

Nagy shares his feelings regarding being bumped out of his scheduled start in Game 7 in favor of Jaret Wright: "As we went through Game 6, I kind of felt like that was the way we were leaning. It was all hands on deck at that point. I had a feeling that was the decision because I had been up in the bullpen several times in Game 6. They made decisions based on what they felt was best for the team, but I still knew I had to be ready. It was Game 7, and all hands were on deck again. It was the full gauntlet of emotions because I was supposed to start and they chose otherwise. Jaret went out and pitched great. I was very excited and happy for him because he deserved it. Jaret gave us a great chance to win Game 7."

Jaret Wright and Florida Marlins starter Al Leiter both held the opposing lineup scoreless through the first two innings. Cleveland got things started in the third when Thome walked and Grissom followed with a single. Jaret Wright laid down a perfect sacrifice bunt and moved both runners into scoring position with only one out. Omar Vizquel failed to score the runners when he popped out to the shortstop. The pressure was then on starting second baseman Tony Fernandez, who came to the plate with two out. Fernandez, a savvy veteran, came up big in the clutch by hitting a two-run single that gave the Indians a 2–0 lead. Thanks in large part to a great pitching effort by Jaret Wright, the 2–0 lead stood until the bottom of the seventh inning, when Bobby Bonilla smashed a solo home run to cut the lead in half. Hargrove justifies his decision to leave in Jaret Wright until the sixth inning: "He was still throwing quite well, and it was just one bad pitch. It was a first-pitch change-up that he left over the plate, and Bobby crushed it. I knew that both Jaret and Sandy thought Bobby was looking for a first-pitch fastball, but it just didn't work out." Wright went six-plus innings and gave up only one run. It was more than anyone in Cleveland could have asked for. Now it was up to the bullpen. Mike Hargrove goes into a bit more detail about the bullpen situation with Mike Jackson and José Mesa: "We rode Mike Jackson really hard, and my pitching coach, Mark Wiley, walked around and talked to our relievers with a little note card. He kept a card with him asking them how much they had thrown and how much they have left going into that night. Mark said that Jackson stated he only had one hitter left in him. So I brought him in the eighth and went to Mesa in the ninth." The Marlins pitchers had been sharp as well, holding the Indians to only two runs heading into the ninth inning.

The Indians would need an insurance run as José Mesa had been shaky in the post-season, and a one-run lead hardly seemed safe. They almost got their wish as two men reached base in the top half of the ninth. With only one out, Sandy Alomar Jr. had a chance to score as he raced home on a ground ball hit to the shortstop. But for some reason, Sandy chose not to slide and was thrown out at home. It may have not seemed like a big mistake at the time, but only minutes later, the inability to score that run became enormous. Hargrove discloses that he never considered having a pinch runner for Sandy Alomar Jr.: "No, Sandy ran pretty well and was our best catcher. He was a large part of the team, and for me, there was no reason to pull him from the game. Not in the seventh game of the series with a one-run lead."

Many stories have been told about the mental condition of José Mesa as he took the mound to try to save the game in the bottom of the ninth, and none of these stories are flattering. On paper, it looked like a foregone conclusion that Mesa would get the save and Cleveland would finally get that long-awaited championship parade. After all, Mesa had been one of the most dominant closers in the game for three straight seasons. As Cleveland Indians fans held their breath, Mesa bounced his first warm-up pitch two feet in front of home plate—and it was all downhill from there.

Moises Alou continued his amazing series by hitting a line-drive single to start the inning. The next batter, Bobby Bonilla, failed to capitalize and struck out. For a moment, it looked like Mesa was only two outs away from giving the Indians the World Series title. Tragically for Cleveland fans, the Indians would not get any closer. Charles Johnson hit a line-drive single to right field that allowed Alou to advance to third base with only one out. Mesa needed a strikeout or a double play to keep the lead. He was unable to get either as Craig Counsell hit a long sacrifice fly to right field that allowed Alou to tag from third and score. The game was tied, and Mesa had blown his third playoff save in a matter of weeks. The game's momentum shifted squarely to Florida. Mike Hargrove shares what happened when Mesa left the mound at the end of the inning, as well as the general mood in the dugout at the time: "I didn't say anything to José, and I never have since. The mood was a downer, and it really took the wind out of our sails after that happened."

It was only appropriate that Charles Nagy would be the one to come out of the bullpen to face the Marlins in the bottom of the eleventh. Nagy had suffered through so many lousy years as the Indians rebuilt, continually fighting to stay positive about the team. Nagy was one of the most beloved Indians of the '90s. Sadly for Nagy, on this evening, he wasn't pitching against the Marlins—he was pitching against destiny.

Bobby Bonilla led off the bottom half of the inning with a single. The next batter, Greg Zaun, failed to execute the bunt and popped out to Nagy. It looked like maybe the Indians were about to catch a break when destiny reared its ugly head yet again. Craig Counsell hit a tailor-made double-play grounder toward Tony Fernandez. The Indians were seconds away from getting out of the jam when Fernandez let it roll between his legs. At that one moment, it seemed as if time stood still. Fernandez had built a reputation as a solid defensive player, and this error was almost unthinkable.

The error was costly as it allowed Bonilla to advance to third base with only one out. Hargrove had no choice but to call for an intentional walk to Eisenreich to load the bases and create a force-out at any base. Tony Fernandez

Tony Fernandez was a sure-handed second baseman—except for one play in Game 7 of the 1997 World Series. Photo by *David DeLuca*.

had the chance for redemption as he fielded the Devon White ground ball and threw out Bonilla at home for the second out. NBC broadcaster Bob Costas accurately said, "And that, ladies and gentlemen, is what it means to be a professional." Fernandez had redeemed himself for the moment, and the Indians were one out away from extending the game. But that one out would never materialize, as Edgar Renteria then hit a soft line drive over the glove of Nagy and through the hole at shortstop to win the game. If the inning had ended differently, Hargrove would have had Nagy come out again for the next inning, but alas, that didn't happen. "Nagy—he was our guy," said Hargrove. It was one of the most painful ways a team could lose a World Series. Hargrove reveals what he said to the team when the game was over: "I told them that I was very proud of them and that we had gone a lot further than anyone thought we would—the usual things you say to people in that situation. It was such a tough situation that nothing you say is going to make it any better. I let them know I was proud of them and that they had played a great ballclub. The Marlins were loaded." However, Hargrove doesn't dwell too much on this pivotal game:

> I don't think about it that often. I had a guy ask me about it about a month after the series was over. He asked me how long it took me to get over it, and I told him that as soon as I got over it I would let him know. Then, about a month ago, someone else asked me, and I repeated, "As soon as I get over it, I will let you know." It has been sixteen years. It is easier not to think about it because I'm like anyone else in that I start playing "what if." I ask myself, "What if Mesa had thrown the fastball in like we wanted to or thrown the slider down and away?" I have no clue why he was so scared of throwing his fastball—I really don't. I know Omar came out and blasted him in his book, but he had saved so many important games for us in the past, including the ALCS clincher by striking out Roberto Alomar.

John Hart, general manager for the Indians, reveals his disappointment over the Game 7 loss:

> I had dinner with Mike the other night, and we both mentioned how we have never gone back and watched Game 7. Time does heal it. I think it may have been more painful for Mike, but it was still painful for me. When we lost Game 5 in '97…it was a terrible game to lose because we wanted to go back to Florida up 3–2 with Chad Ogea facing Kevin Brown. I remember after Ogea had a great game and we won, I walked onto the roof

*at the Fawn Blue Hotel later that night and thought, "This is Game 7." I remember '95 as a great experience, and we had a great team, but I had to come to grips with winning or losing. We had done everything we could do, and we just had to go play the game. When you turn the ball over to José Mesa, who had saved so many games and without whom we wouldn't have gotten there...but it ended up tied.*

*Before Mesa blew the save, they called us out of the stands because it was Major League protocol for the wining team's owner and GM to be in the locker room. So we watched the rest of the game in Grover's office. It was painful to watch the rest of the game in the bowels of Joe Robbie Stadium as our team eventually lost. I was devastated, but Dick said to me that we gave it our best, and then he waited and greeted the players as they came in from the field. He told each player he was proud of him and that we would get 'em next year.*

Charles Nagy had the following to say about the devastating loss: "I can still picture the ball being hit—he didn't hit it very well. I thought it was hit harder than it was. It was one of those balls that just kind of knuckled in and tipped off my glove. To this day, I still wish I had caught that ball. It was Game 7, and going into the ninth inning, everyone in the bullpen was getting ready to storm the field for the celebration. The next thing you know, it was like, 'Grab your glove and get ready to go into the game.' It just didn't happen for us."

Jim Thome also discusses the heartbreak of the loss: "It was very hard to get that close in the last game—talk about the emotional high to the emotional low. There is nothing worse in sports than losing a Game 7."

It was clear to me after speaking with Nagy, Thome, Hart and Hargrove that the Game 7 loss is going to hurt for a long time to come. However, it wasn't from any lack of strategy, hustle or hard work. It was a great group of ballplayers and a fine class of people. Sometimes in baseball—and in life—the ball just doesn't bounce the right way. But maybe, just maybe, it will next time.

## Chapter 4

# GROVER'S LAST RIDE

The Indians got about as close as a team could without actually winning the World Series in the fall of 1997. It made Cleveland fans hunger for a championship even more, now believing that it truly was possible. The job of Hart was to obtain what seemingly was a missing piece without losing too much in return. The team parted with veterans Orel Hershiser, Tony Fernandez and Bip Roberts. All three had high and low moments in the 1997 playoff run, but it was the lowest ones that stuck out.

Matt Williams, who had a great 1997 season on the field, encountered some personal problems off the field that led to him asking for a trade. The Indians found a trade partner with the Arizona Diamondbacks and were able to obtain veteran third baseman Travis Fryman in the deal for Williams. Fryman would become a fan favorite for many years, eventually landing a coaching job in the Indians organization when his playing days were over.

Kenny Lofton, who had been dealt to the Atlanta Braves the previous season, was now on his way back to Cleveland. It was an early Christmas present for Cleveland Indians fans everywhere on December 8, 1997, when Lofton agreed to a contract to return to the team. Kenny explains his decision to come back to Cleveland: "First of all, I didn't want to leave. But I did get the chance to return. I was given the chance by assistant general manager Dan O'Dowd. We had the conversation in the off-season, and he understood how I felt. We worked out a situation for me to come back to Cleveland—if it wasn't for him, it wouldn't have happened."

The Indians got off to a hot start and won their first six games, all on the road, to start the season. They remained hot and closed out the first two months with a 33-22 record. They seemed to have gotten past the heartbreak of the prior season and were cruising to their fourth straight division title.

The Indians continued to dominate the division, and they held a 50-35 record heading into the All Star break. They once again sent several players to the Midsummer Classic: first baseman Jim Thome, center fielder Kenny Lofton, shortstop Omar Vizquel, right fielder Manny Ramirez, pitcher Bartolo Colón and catcher Sandy Alomar Jr. It was another proud moment when Cleveland fans witnessed their pregame introductions.

Cleveland won the division with a final record of 89-73 after holding a double-digit lead almost the entire second half of the season. Jaret Wright, who had high hopes cast on him after his incredible rookie campaign, produced only mediocre results, finishing with a 12-10 record and a 4.72 ERA. Bartolo Colón finished with fourteen wins, while Nagy and Burba tied for the team lead with fifteen wins each. Mike Jackson, who took over the closing duties from Mesa, finished with an incredible 1.55 ERA and forty saves.

The Indians' first-round opponent that season was a familiar foe: the Boston Red Sox. The Red Sox were making their return to the playoffs for the first time since Cleveland knocked them out in '95. They had a few years of built-up frustration that they hoped to take out on the Cleveland ballclub.

Boston sent their ace, Pedro Martinez, to the mound to face Jaret Wright in front of a sold-out crowd at Jacobs Field. Wright was coming off of a subpar season, but Hargrove remained confident in him because of the post-season brilliance he had shown the prior year.

It was quickly apparent that Wright would not have the magic of the prior season as he fell behind early. Mo Vaughn hit a three-run home run for Boston in the first, putting the Sox ahead to stay. In the fifth inning, Nomar Garciaparra hit a three-run shot of his own and expanded the lead to 6-0. Mo Vaughn wasn't done as he hit a two-run home run in the top half of the sixth, increasing Boston's lead to 8-0. Lofton smashed a two-run home run of his own in the bottom half of the sixth; however, the Indians never got any closer and eventually lost 11-3. The win ended a thirteen-game losing streak for the Red Sox. It was their first playoff win since the epic Bill Buckner error of the 1986 World Series against the New York Mets.

Dwight Gooden was called on in Game 2 for the Indians and was set to face knuckleballer Tim Wakefield. Nomar Garciaparra put the Red Sox up 2-0 after doubling in Lewis and Valentin. Shortly afterward, Cleveland manager Mike Hargrove and Dwight Gooden were ejected from the game

Sandy Alomar Jr. was a beloved veteran behind the plate and in the clubhouse. *Photo by Don McKee.*

for arguing with the umpires about a play at the plate. Gooden was replaced by Dave Burba, who went on to pitch a solid game. David Justice cut the lead in half by hitting a sacrifice fly that scored Lofton in the bottom of the first. Then the Indians tied it when Sandy Alomar Jr. doubled in Brian Giles in the bottom of the second. After Joey Cora walked, Lofton doubled in Alomar to give the Indians the lead. Wakefield left the game, and with two out, David Justice hit a three-run home run to put the Indians ahead 6–2. Garciaparra drove in a run for Boston in the third, but an Alomar double scored Travis Fryman to make it 7–3 Indians. The Red Sox did their best to narrow the gap, but the Indians hung on to win 9–5 and even up the series.

Game 3 saw the series move to Fenway Park in Boston. On the mound for the Indians would be veteran right-hander and fan favorite Charles Nagy. His opponent on the Red Sox was Bret Saberhagen. It was a closely contested game that saw Boston grab the early lead in the bottom half of the fourth on a sacrifice groundout. The Indians responded by hitting four solo home runs in the next five innings. Two of the solo bombs came off the bat of Manny Ramirez. Jim Thome and Kenny Lofton also had one each, and the Indians took Game 3 by a score of 4–3.

Bartolo Colón was given the ball to start Game 4 against Pete Schourek. The game started off as a pitchers' duel, with neither team scoring through the first three innings. In the fourth, Nomar Garciaparra homered to put the Red Sox up 1–0. They held the lead until the eighth, when Kenny Lofton and Omar Vizquel singled with one out. Justice then doubled to center, scoring both Lofton and Vizquel to put the Indians ahead 2–1. Mike Jackson held on to the lead in the bottom of the ninth, and the Indians won the game and series. It was a strong start to the playoff run for the Indians as they managed to come from behind during three straight games to take the series.

In 1998, no team in baseball could come close to the numbers being put up by the Yankees. They won an amazing 114 games and took their division by 22 games. Their record and lineup had people around baseball comparing them to the historic 1927 Yankees. They would be waiting to face Cleveland fresh off a three-game sweep of the Texas Rangers.

Jaret Wright was again called on to start a Game 1 for the Indians. This game was much like his prior start against Boston as the young Wright was lit up by Yankee batters—he couldn't even get out of the first inning. By the time Wright was pulled for veteran Chad Ogea, the Yankees were up 5–0. Despite a late inning home run by Manny Ramirez, this game was all Yankees, who won by a final score of 7–2. The starter for the Yankees, David Wells, had another masterful night against the Indians.

Game 2 saw twenty-game winner David Cone start for the Yankees against Charles Nagy for Cleveland. David Justice smacked a solo home run in the fourth, giving the Indians the early 1–0 lead. It was the first time the Yankees trailed in a game that post-season. A Scott Brosius double tied the game in the seventh, but the Yankees were unable to score him. They would waste many other chances to score that game. The game remained close and moved to extra innings. Jim Thome led off the top of the twelfth with a single. Enrique Wilson was brought in to pinch-run for Thome. Up next was Travis Fryman, who laid down a sacrifice bunt. As Yankee pitcher Jeff Nelson went to throw the ball to first, he hit Fryman, and the ball rolled past second baseman Chuck Knoblauch, who was covering first on the play. Knoblauch tried to argue the call as the ball continued to roll. Wilson and Fryman continued to run, and Wilson would eventually score on the live ball. It was a huge mental mistake on the part of Knoblauch. An error by Tino Martinez then put Fryman at third. The Indians now had the lead back. They would score two more times to increase the lead and hang on to win the game, evening up the series at a game apiece.

Game 3 proved to be a gem by Cleveland starter Bartolo Colón. After allowing an RBI single to Bernie Williams in the first, he bounced back to throw a complete-game four-hit masterpiece. As Colón was mowing down batters at the plate, the Indians offense continued to stay hot by hitting multiple home runs. Jim Thome had two more home runs, combined with homers by Manny Ramirez and Mark Whitten. The Indians cruised to a 6–1 victory and took a 2-1 lead in the series.

There was a lot of drama surrounding New York's Game 4 starter. Orlando "El Duque" Hernandez was the older brother of the previous year's World Series nemesis, Livan Hernandez. The former had come to the Yankees covered in mystery, having defected from Cuba just ten months earlier. Both pitching staffs kept it a low-hitting affair as the game saw a total of only eight hits. Hernandez shut down the Indians all night long, however, and the Yankees took Game 4 by a score of 4–0 to even up the series.

The Indians turned to their veteran Chad Ogea to get things back on track for the pivotal Game 5. They skipped Jaret Wright's start but quickly went back to him after Ogea got shelled early. Ogea gave up three in the first, and the Indians were never able to dig out of the hole. The Yankees used the early lead along with another strong start from David Wells to cruise to a 5–3 win and take a commanding series lead back to New York.

The pitching matchup for Game 6 was David Cone against Charles Nagy. The Yankees built a 6–0 lead behind David Cone, but the Indians refused to go quietly. A bases-loaded walk and a grand slam by Jim Thome made it 6–5 in the fifth. The Yankees responded by scoring three more runs on a Derek Jeter triple and a Bernie Williams single to make it 9–5. Mariano Rivera had no issues closing things out in the top of the ninth, and the Indians quest to return to the World Series came up short.

It was a fine season with many highs, but it lacked the magic of the 1997 post-season. The Indians knew that another strong off-season was necessary if they wanted to contend with highly powered teams such as the Yankees, who eventually went on to win the World Series in a four-game sweep of the San Diego Padres.

The major move of the off-season came when the Indians signed free-agent All Star second baseman and future Hall of Famer Roberto Alomar. In previous years, Alomar had been the league's best second baseman, both with his glove and his bat. Before his playing days were over, he would receive ten Gold Glove awards, more than any second baseman in Major League Baseball history. He had a sensational bat to go with his excellent glove, winning four Silver Slugger awards as well. Along with his immense talent, he brought with him the two World Series rings he had won in Toronto. He was the best in the game, and many thought he was the one who could finally get Cleveland over the hump. The Indians had had a revolving door at second base since the Baerga trade, and this was seen as a more permanent solution.

The Indians jumped out to an 8-1 start and never looked back. By the time the season was over, they had won an impressive 97 games and

Robbie Alomar was a major free-agent signing heading into the 1999 season. *Photo by Kim Murphy.*

scored 1,009 runs. They spent a whopping 158 days in first place and won the division by 21.5 games. Cleveland was a force with which few teams could contend. Hargrove had led his team to the playoffs for the fifth straight year as the Indians captured their fifth straight American League Central Division championship. Jacobs Field again led all of baseball in attendance, selling out the entire season for the fifth straight year.

Bartolo Colón took the next step in becoming the team's outright ace as he won eighteen games. Colón had plenty of support in the rotation, with Charles Nagy winning seventeen games and Dave Burba chipping in with fifteen of his own. Closer Mike Jackson again looked strong, saving thirty-nine games.

The Indians were a force to be reckoned with as they entered the playoffs. Standing in their way were their old rivals: the Boston Red Sox. Cleveland had plenty of recent playoff experience against Boston and looked to continue its winning ways. But Boston was no slouch, having won ninety-four games that year and finishing second only because they played in the AL Eastern Division led by the powerful ninety-eight-win New York Yankees.

Boston's ace was Pedro Martinez, a perennial CY Young candidate coming off his best season as a pro. Martinez had won twenty-three games and boasted a minuscule ERA of 2.07. The matchup between him and Bartolo Colón in Game 1 had all the makings of a classic. Both pitchers were highly regarded as the best in their league, and this was their chance to showcase their skill in front of a packed house at Jacobs Field and a nationwide audience watching at home.

Boston obtained an early 1–0 lead with a leadoff home run by Nomar Garciaparra in the second inning. Garciaparra also helped score the second run for the Red Sox when he led off the fourth inning with a double and then scored on Mike Stanley's RBI single. Pedro Martinez was lights out until he had to leave the game due to injury in the bottom of the fifth inning and was replaced by Derek Lowe. This was a huge break for the Indians because Martinez had looked untouchable up until that point. The Indians would tie the game in the bottom of the sixth with a two-run home run by Jim Thome. Colón managed to settle down and dominate the Red Sox hitters the rest of the way, striking out eleven in eight innings. In the bottom of the ninth, the Indians called on their Jacobs Field magic one more time when Travis Fryman hit a game-winning bases-loaded single off Boston reliever Rich Garcés. The Indians had scratched and clawed their way to an impressive Game 1 victory.

Game 2 would provide little to no drama as the Indians blew out the Red Sox by a score of 11–1. They used sharp pitching by Charles Nagy and powerful hitting from everyone in the lineup. Harold Baines had a three-run home run in the third to make it 6–1, and then Jim Thome smashed a grand slam in the fourth to put the game completely out of reach. The Indians were rolling as they headed to Fenway Park to try and put the series away.

Game 3 was the point in the series when Mike Hargrove began to make a series of moves that would lead to his eventual dismissal as manager. Dave Burba had been shutting out the Red Sox for four innings when he left with a strained forearm. Mike Hargrove chose to insert presumed Game 4 starter Jaret Wright instead of rookie middle reliever Sean DePaula. The Red Sox captured a 2–1 lead off Wright in the fifth on a single and sacrifice fly. Cleveland would tie it in the top of the sixth before Boston scored again to go back up 3–2. The Indians again showed their willingness to fight as they scored to tie it 3–3 heading into the bottom of the seventh inning.

John Valentin hit a bases-loaded double off of Ricardo Rincón that put the Red Sox up 5–3. Brian Daubach then followed with a three-run home run, and the game was quickly out of reach. The Red Sox went on to win the game 9–3, and the momentum had swiftly switched sides.

With presumed starter Jaret Wright being used in relief the previous day, and no emergency starter on the playoff roster, the Indians had no other option but to start Bartolo Colón on three days' rest for the first time in his career. Neither he nor the bullpen could stop the onslaught of Red Sox runs. Colón was tagged for seven runs in fewer than two innings, and the relievers didn't fare much better. The Sox drove in a total of twenty-three in the game, a blowout from the second inning on. The series was headed back to Cleveland with the Indians' hopes on life support.

Game 5 of the 1999 American League Division Series between the Cleveland Indians and Boston Red Sox took place on October 11, 1999. It became an instant classic. Sorely for Cleveland fans, it became a classic for all the wrong reasons. The Indians called on their veteran starter Charles Nagy in the hopes of avoiding the epic collapse. Facing him was Brett Saberhagen, who had been lit up in his Game 2 start. Due to injury and other staff issues, both pitchers were pitching on only three days' rest.

Nomar Garciaparra hit a two-run home run off of Nagy in the top half of the first to give Boston the early lead. Cleveland responded quickly in the bottom half of the inning with a Vizquel RBI double and a two-run home run by Jim Thome. It was the third home run of the series for Thome, and it put the Indians ahead 3–2 going into the second inning.

Nagy looked impressive in the top half of the second as he set down the Boston lineup in order. Travis Fryman kept the Indians bats hot as he hit a two-run home run with Will Cordero on base to give the Indians a 5–2 advantage. The home run also knocked Saberhagen from the game.

Things were setting up nicely for Nagy as he took the mound up 5–2 to start the third, but it all came crashing down quickly. He showed that he wasn't ready to be pitching on such short rest and surrendered the lead back to Boston in brutal fashion. He gave up five runs on three hits, the biggest being a grand slam by Troy O'Leary. Boston took a 7–5 lead and chased Nagy from the game.

The Indians refused to stay down for very long. Doubles from Roberto Alomar and Manny Ramirez followed by another Jim Thome home run gave them back the lead at 8–7. The fans who filled Jacobs Field that evening were seeing a slugfest between two heavyweight prizefighters. Boston used a sacrifice fly by John Valentin in the top half of the fourth and tied the game once again.

As Boston took the field for the bottom half of the fourth, a very interesting thing occurred. Boston manager Jimmy Williams decided to replace Derek Lowe with the hurting Pedro Martinez, who had left Game 1 with a back injury. This decision would prove to be a smart one, as Pedro pitched spectacularly, throwing six hitless innings while striking out eight and walking three.

As Martinez was shutting down the Indians lineup, Cleveland responded with rookie reliever Sean DePaula. DePaula, whom Hargrove had declined to use in Game 3, wrecking his rotation as a result, matched Pedro for three

The Indians sold out 455 straight games from 1995 to 2001. *Courtesy of Clock and Tickers Inc.*

innings. Despite his success, Hargrove removed DePaula and opted to use inconsistent setup man Paul Shuey for the seventh inning. The decision immediately backfired when Troy O'Leary hit a three-run home run to put Boston ahead for good. The life was instantly sucked out of Jacobs Field as O'Leary rounded the bases. Pedro Martinez finished his brilliance by keeping the Indians hitless for the sixth consecutive inning in the bottom of the ninth, sending the Indians fans home stunned and saddened.

Boston would go on to lose in five games to the eventual World Series champion New York Yankees in the ALCS. The one victory for Boston in that series was a Pedro Martinez win over Roger Clemens. Meanwhile, back in Cleveland, the off-season had already begun and the unthinkable was about to happen.

Chapter 5

# A NEW VOICE

On October 15, 1999, Cleveland Indians fans were saddened and stunned when John Hart fired Mike Hargrove. Hargrove had amassed more than seven hundred victories and led his team to five straight division titles, including two trips to the World Series. He took a team that was viewed as a constant loser and made it into a Major League powerhouse. It came as a surprise to Hargrove as well, who told cnnsi.com, "It's hard for me to say if I'm paying the price. I don't know that this would have happened if we had gone further into the playoffs."

John Hart said, "The team needed a new voice that could get them to the next level." Hart claimed that it wasn't a single event that caused the firing. Many feel that it was how poorly Hargrove handled the rotation and pitching staff in the 1999 playoffs that led to his firing. The Indians pitching staff allowed forty-four runs in the final three games of the series. Hargrove was quoted as saying, "I didn't pitch in the twenty-three-run game—I don't think I've been set up as the fall guy. We just didn't get the job done in the post-season, and somebody has to be responsible. And I'm responsible for that." When Hart was questioned about the cause of the firing, he said, "There is a need for a new energy, a new voice, coming from the clubhouse; this change will create a different atmosphere." The fact that Hart claimed a new voice was needed after Hargrove had sustained success for so long was a head-scratcher to many. As quoted by cnnsi.com, Hargrove went on to say, "I enjoyed my time here—we're still going to live in Cleveland. There may be some people who don't like that."

Cleveland fans were shocked by the firing of Mike Hargrove. *Photo by Dr. Gosky.*

Charles Nagy gives his view as to why the move was made and how it impacted the team: "They decided to make that change for whatever reason, and it was one of those things that is part of the game. Grover and I have a great relationship, and we still talk to this day. It was disappointing and sad to see that happen. They felt a change was needed, but they didn't go outside the organization to hire anyone different because we all loved Charlie. He is a great guy."

After the shocking firing of Mike Hargrove, the pressure was on Hart to pick the perfect replacement. He felt he did when he hired Charlie Manuel as the thirty-seventh manager in Cleveland Indians history. The move was made in the hopes it would be easier for players and fans to adjust because Manuel had been around the team for so many years.

Kenny Lofton discusses his reaction to the switch at manager: "Charlie Manuel had been around for so long that everyone respected John Hart's decision. It was more of a transition and understanding that it was a business decision. We had to understand that sometimes in baseball, they make moves that just don't make any sense, and that was one of them. They put in a guy with Charlie Manuel who everyone loved and respected, so it was an easy transition for us because Charlie was already in the organization."

*Right*: Charlie Manuel took over as manager in 2000. *Courtesy of LaNasas Barbershop.*

*Below*: New manager Charlie Manuel talks with star first baseman Jim Thome. *Courtesy of LaNasas Barbershop.*

Jim Thome shares his reaction to the stunning move: "I think Mike did a great job and was a guy we fed off. He had some great teams but sadly was let go. They replaced him with a great baseball man. I think on the business end of it, it's hard to see moves like that made. But in the end, you just hope the moves that are made benefit the team."

Chuck Finley was brought in to help the starting rotation. *Courtesy of LaNasas Barbershop.*

The switch from Hargrove to Manuel wasn't the only big move of the 2000 season. Dick Jacobs sold the team to Larry Dolan for $323 million. As part of the deal, Dolan bought all of the stock at just over $12 a share, making the franchise privately held once again. Dolan had grown up in Cleveland and attended St. Ignatius High School. He attended college at the University of Notre Dame, where he earned an LLB degree in 1956. After leaving Notre Dame, Larry served for two years in the U.S. Marine Corps, where he attained the rank of first lieutenant. After leaving the military, he served as an assistant prosecutor in Geauga County and then opened up his own private practice. He went on to become president and managing partner of Thrasher, Dinsmore & Dolan.

The big free-agent signing was that of starting pitcher Chuck Finley, who had made a great name for himself while playing with the California Angels. When he left the Angels, he held the all-time wins mark for the club. He was very popular, and a good left-handed starter was always a plus for any rotation.

The Indians opened 2000 on the road against the Baltimore Orioles. Normally, this matchup would have the normal hype of Opening Day; however, this time it had added build to it because of the man sitting in the dugout calling the shots for Baltimore. Mike Hargrove had taken over as manager in Baltimore, and it was the first time in modern history in which a manager faced his old team to start the following season after being fired.

Opening Day provided the pitching matchup most were hoping to see when Bartolo Colón took the mound to face Oriole ace Mike Mussina. It proved to be the pitching duel most anticipated, and the Indians won their first game under Manuel against their former manager 4–1. It was also the first game for new closer Steve Karsay. Mike Jackson had left the team in the off-season to go to the Philadelphia Phillies.

May got off to a horrible start as the Tribe dropped their first six games of the month. They were able to turn it around with a couple three-game winning streaks, including a sweep of the Kansas City Royals. They continued to be up and down and closed out May with a record of 27-22. Normally, the Central Division was weak and that record would have been good enough for first place, but this season was different because the Chicago White Sox were off to a red-hot start and led the division by 1.5 games.

Second place was unfamiliar territory for the Indians, and it showed as June turned into a horrible month. They hit a six-game losing skid early in the month and followed it with two three-game losing streaks later in the month. By the time June ended, they were 40-38 and 9.5 games out of first place. The hitting was going well, but they could not get consistent starting pitching. Injuries had ravaged the Indians rotation, which led to unknowns such as Kane Davis being called up as emergency starters who simply were not ready to perform on the big-league level.

On June 29, John Hart waved what many considered to be a white flag when he traded away power hitter David Justice to the New York Yankees for Zach Day, Rickey Ledee and Jake Westbrook. While Ledee and Day never went on to anything of note, Westbrook later became a key member of the rotation. It was the first sign of a possible youth movement that Hart had been trying to initiate. Richie Sexson would now replace Justice as the starting left fielder, with Manny Ramirez in right and Kenny Lofton in center.

As July came to a close, the Indians remained 11.5 games behind the White Sox. With the deficit growing, John Hart felt it was time to make another move. Hart surprised many when he traded away Richie Sexson, Kane Davis and Paul Rigdon to the Milwaukee Brewers for starting pitcher Jason Bere, noted closer Bob Wickman and Steve Woodard. It was a puzzling move to many because Karsay was doing fine as a closer, and Sexson had recently been promoted as the starting left fielder after the Justice trade.

The Indians responded well to the trade as they went on a six-game winning streak in early August. They were known for heating up in the summer months and would have to once again if they hoped to catch Chicago in the standings. Bob Wickman saved eight games in August as the new closer despite looking shaky in most of them. Wickman actually lost two games in August as well, which kept fans nervous every time he took the mound. They finished the month a season-high 10 games over .500 with a record of 70-60. They remained in second place but had cut Chicago's lead down to 7.5 games.

As September began and Chicago refused to cool down, it became apparent that the Indians would not win their sixth consecutive division title. Instead, they set their sights on chasing down the wildcard berth. They were trailing both Seattle and Oakland but were confident they could overtake them for the final spot.

The Indians ended up winning an impressive ninety games that year. In most seasons, that would be enough to win a division or the wildcard spot. But this season was different because Seattle had won ninety-one games, leaving Cleveland out of the playoffs for the first time since 1994.

After Albert Belle left in 1996, fans felt it was crucial for the Indians not to allow another power hitter to walk away in free agency. Manny Ramirez had been a consistent All Star and heavy hitter in the lineup since being called up to the big-league roster in late 1993. He was a key piece of the championship runs in the mid- to late '90s. Ramirez was known for his lazy play in the field and bone-headed base running mistakes, but because of his bat, the Indians and many other teams were willing to look the other way.

With many in the media and front office feeling that it was only a matter of time before Ramirez resigned with the Indians, it came as a surprise when he decided to sign with Boston instead. Ramirez was now a member of the Red Sox, and Cleveland had been burned once again by their best hitter leaving for greener pastures.

Ellis Burks was in the twilight of his career, but the Indians remained confident he could fill the gap left by Ramirez when they signed him as a free agent. A few weeks after the Burks signing, they brought in Marty Cordova. Marty had played most of his career with the Twins and was seen as a solid pickup for a corner outfielder role.

The signings of Cordova and Burks were helpful, but the Indians still needed that one major bat to replace Manny Ramirez. On January 9, 2001, they thought they found it when they signed Juan Gonzalez, who

Manny Ramirez left for greener pastures after the 2000 season. *Photo by Dr. Gosky.*

had played the first ten years of his career with the Texas Rangers and had consistently been one of their best players. He blasted forty-plus home runs five separate times and hit thirty-nine in 1999. In 2000, however, he made the costly mistake of going to Detroit and playing Comerica Park, where he saw his numbers plummet in the pitcher-friendly stadium. It was a one-year contract, and Gonzalez was determined to return to his power-hitting ways.

Opening Day did not go well as David Wells and the Chicago White Sox came to town and cruised to a 7–4 victory over Bartolo Colón. The date was Monday, April 2, 2001, and it was the 455th straight sellout at Jacobs Field. It was special because it was the last game of the streak, which had started on June 12, 1995, and seemed as though it would never end. The next night against Chicago, the attendance was reported as 32,763, a respectable number but not the customary sellout that everyone had come to expect. The Indians won the game, however, and went on to have a good first month. They finished April with a 14-9 record, highlighted by a six-game winning streak late in the month.

The Indians continued their streak in May, eventually winning ten straight games. Rookie pitcher Sabathia continued to look strong and pile up wins of his own as the Indians remained in the thick of the early playoff race. They finished up May with a 33-17 record, only one game back of the Minnesota Twins for first place in the division. CC Sabathia was 5-2 and looking stronger each time out.

The Indians hit a snag in mid-June when they went on a five-game losing streak. Later on in the month, they went on another four-game losing streak.

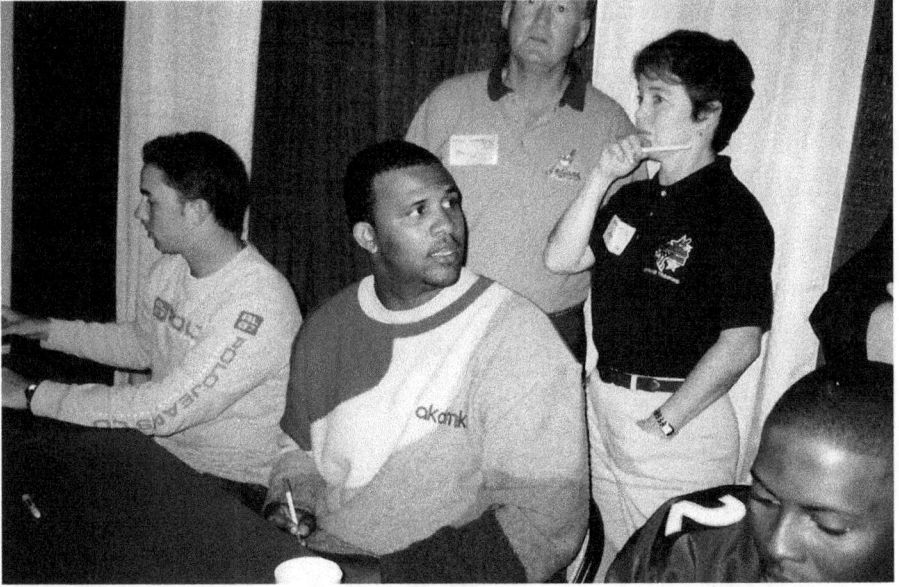

CC Sabathia (center) joined the team in 2000 and was a force for many years. *Courtesy of LaNasas Barbershop.*

It was a June swoon, but they still managed to snap out of it and finish the month with a record of 45-32 and only two games back of first place.

Sunday, August 5, 2001, would go down as one of the wildest games in Jacobs Field history. The sellout crowd that evening was about to witness a *Sunday Night Baseball* classic. The eleven-inning masterpiece featured twenty-nine runs and forty combined hits. It took four hours and eleven minutes to play and had to be seen to be believed. The Seattle Mariners came into Jacobs Field as the hottest team in baseball with an incredible 80-31 record. It was a blistering pace that had many believing they could set the all-time win mark.

On the mound that evening for Cleveland was Dave Burba, while Aaron Sele took the bump for Seattle. The Seattle batters began to heat up after a scoreless first inning by scoring four runs in the top of the second. Doubles by Martin, Cameron and Lampkin did the majority of the damage before Ichiro Suzuki singled to make it 4–0 Seattle. The Indians were unable to answer with any runs in the bottom of the inning.

The top of the third became a nightmare for Cleveland as Seattle exploded for eight runs. The amazing thing about the eight-run outburst was that none of the runs were the result of a home run. Seattle used clutch hitting to knock starter Dave Burba out of the game. Pitching in relief for Cleveland was Mike Bacsik, who gave up four of the hits, walked a batter and hit a batter. By the end of the inning, Seattle had scored eight times on seven hits, one error and one hit batsman. It was 12–0 Seattle on national television.

Cleveland got on the scoreboard in the bottom of the fourth inning when Jim Thome hit a two-run home run off of Aaron Sele. The Indians had held Seattle scoreless in the top half of the inning, so this made the score 12–2. Seattle promptly answered the Thome home run with two runs of their own in the top half of the fifth inning, extending the lead to 14–2.

Russell Branyan started off the bottom of the seventh with a solo home run. Branyan was known for his power—and the high ratio of strikeouts that went along with it. The Indians managed to score two more times before the inning was over, cutting the lead to 14–5. The other two runs came courtesy of a Jolbert Cabrera two-run single.

The rally continued in the bottom of the eighth when the Indians used home runs by Thome and Marty Cordova to cut into the lead. An Omar Vizquel RBI double later in the inning cut the lead to 14–9 and gave Indians fans some hope heading into the ninth inning.

The Indians bullpen was able to keep the score 14–9 heading into the bottom of the ninth inning. Ed Taubensee hit a bloop single to center to start the rally. But after a Jim Thome fly out and a Russell Branyan strikeout, the Indians were down to their final out still trailing by five runs. A Marty Cordova double kept hopes alive and put two runners in scoring position for Will Cordero. Cordero drew a walk against Jeff Nelson to load the bases, bringing Einar Diaz to the plate.

Diaz proved to be a clutch hitter when he smashed a two-run single to bring the score to 14–11. Kenny Lofton kept the rally alive by hitting a single into shallow left field to load the bases. This brought Vizquel to the plate with a chance to tie or win the game. Vizquel smashed a Sasaki pitch to the wall in right field that was deep enough to clear the bases and tie the game 14–14. The Vizquel triple was one of the most memorable moments of the 2001 season. Sasaki managed to get out the inning by forcing Jolbert Cabrera to ground out.

The Indians continued the magical comeback in the bottom of the eleventh when Lofton and Vizquel hit line-drive singles to set the table for a dramatic finish. Cabrera then hit a José Paniagua fastball to shallow left field, scoring Lofton and completing the miracle comeback. The Indians had won 15–14 in one of the most memorable and improbable comebacks in baseball history. That it happened on national television against the best team in the league made the victory that much sweeter for Cleveland.

The Indians carried the energy from the big comeback win into August as they went on several winning streaks and finished the month at 76-58. The mark was good enough for first place in the division and 5.5 games up on second-place Minnesota. They kept the momentum rolling in September and won the Central Division for the sixth time in seven years. They finished with a record of 91-71 and were set to face familiar foe Seattle in the first round of the playoffs. The Indians scored 897 runs while letting up 821. Jacobs Field was third in overall attendance in the American League, with 3,175,523 for the season.

The Tribe's starting rotation was shaky at times but featured two solid arms at the top. Bartolo Colón finished 14-12 with a 4.09 ERA, while rookie sensation CC Sabathia lived up to the hype with an incredible 17-5 record along with a 4.39 ERA. Jim Thome smacked a career high in home runs with forty-nine. Thome also had 124 RBIs and batted .291. Juan Gonzalez made the most out of his one season in Cleveland, belting thirty-five home runs and 140 RBIs. Roberto Alomar was once again solid as he finished with thirty stolen bases and a .336 batting average. Ellis Burks fulfilled expectations set for him as he had twenty-eight home runs to go along with 74 RBIs. Marty Cordova also proved to be a smart pickup, batting .301 with twenty home runs and 69 RBIs. Cleveland may have been on its last legs as far as being a dominant team, but it had enough left in the tank to challenge deep into the post-season.

The Seattle Mariners had won 116 regular-season games and came into the first round of the playoffs against Cleveland as a heavy favorite. Manager Lou Piniella had his team ready for a run at the pennant and beyond. Bartolo Colón was called on to start another Game 1 for the Cleveland Indians. His last playoff outing was the blowout loss to the Boston Red Sox in the 1999 divisional playoff. This game would move in a drastically different direction as Colón pitched a gem, going eight innings without giving up any runs. He gave up six hits but also struck out ten Seattle batters. It was this masterful performance combined with a three-run explosion off of Seattle starting pitcher Freddy Garcia in the fourth inning that set the tone for victory. An Einar Diaz RBI single in the sixth added an insurance run, and that was more than enough for the Indians to win. Bob Wickman closed it out in the ninth, and the Indians took Game 1 at Safeco Field by a final score of 4–0.

Seattle coupled a four-run first inning with a dominant pitching performance from Jamie Moyer to take Game 2 by the score of 5-1. Moyer used a variety of breaking balls to keep the Indians hitters guessing all night. Indians starter Chuck Finley continued to be a disappointment, giving another poor start.

The series returned to Jacobs Field for the all-important Game 3 of the series. CC Sabathia was set to make his first playoff start against Aaron Sele. The Indians used an incredible six-hit night from shortstop Omar Vizquel along with many other clutch hits from top to bottom to win 17–2. Home runs by Jim Thome, Juan Gonzalez and Kenny Lofton were just the cherries on top of a giant victory sundae for Cleveland.

Bartolo Colón took the hill in Game 4 at Jacobs Field with a chance to close out the series. For the first six innings, it looked as though he would do exactly that as he took a 1–0 lead into the seventh inning. Up to that point, Colón had pitched fourteen straight scoreless innings in the series. A Juan Gonzalez solo home run had given the Indians a 1–0 lead earlier in the game. But Colón ran into some trouble in the top of the seventh inning. He loaded the bases with no outs before forcing Al Martin to ground out to Jim Thome, who threw home to get the lead runner and keep the game at 1–0 with one out. With the bases still loaded, former Indian David Bell hit a sacrifice fly to tie the game at 1–1 with two outs.

Sensing his starter was tiring, Charlie Manuel called time and visited Colón on the mound. Not much was said as Colón was well past his pitch count, but Manuel felt that his ace had enough left in him to continue. Manuel's decision backfired as Colón promptly gave up back-to-back singles to Suzuki and McLemore that put Seattle ahead 3–1. As Manuel walked back to the mound to pull Colón from the game, he could only second-guess himself for leaving his starter in a few batters too long. The Indians went on to lose the game 6–2, and the series was headed back to Safeco Field in Seattle for a decisive Game 5.

The outcome of Game 5 would be decided on two horrible first-pitch-swinging, lazy double-play balls hit into by Roberto Alomar. Both groundouts proved to be fatal as the Indians could muster only one run against Seattle ace Jamie Moyer. Home plate umpire Mark Hirshbeck squeezed Cleveland starting pitcher Chuck Finley all game and would not call a strike for him unless the pitch was right down the center of the plate. On the contrary, Hirshbeck called everything that left Moyer's hand a strike, no matter where the ball traveled across home plate. Hirshbeck made a joke out of the strike zone, and the Indians batters never had a chance because of it. The bizarre strike zone combined with Alomar's blunders caused the Indians to lose 3–1.

The most frustrating and puzzling part was that, for years, Roberto Alomar had been the Indians' best hitter and smartest player. His strange decisions and lazy baserunning in this pivotal Game 5 would result in his being shipped out of town in the off-season as the sign of a rebuilding project set to begin.

# Chapter 6

# REBUILDING

S ome of the worst words for any sports fan to hear are "rebuilding process." For many years, the Indians were one of the most dominant teams in baseball. They had one of the highest payrolls in baseball and had finished at the top of their division routinely since 1994. A lack of money was never an issue when Dick Jacobs owned the team. When Larry Dolan bought the team, baseball was in a transition process, and small-market owners had to start cracking down on payroll. The 2001 playoff run seemed to be the last with the core group of players from the late '90s as the team entered into a transition process of their own.

The man in charge of the rebuilding process would be new general manager Mark Shapiro, who had been John Hart's assistant since coming to Cleveland in 1992. Hart had left for Texas, so it would be Shapiro's task to work with the new money restrictions and build for the future. Shapiro was seen as a bright baseball mind and was respected by his peers.

The Indians outfield would have a completely different look from years prior as Marty Cordova, Kenny Lofton and Juan Gonzalez all left in free agency. Gonzalez returned to Texas, where he had spent the bulk of his career. Marty Cordova, who had a good season in Cleveland, left for Baltimore and was out of baseball completely only two seasons later. Kenny Lofton signed with the Chicago White Sox, though it was a move not of his choosing.

Lofton explains why he wanted to stay in Cleveland and why he was upset that he had to leave in free agency: "Once again, it wasn't my choice to leave Cleveland. They didn't want me, and they had already decided that it was

Mark Shapiro was the man in charge of the rebuilding process. *Photo by Richard Masci.*

time for me to move on. It wasn't my decision. At the time, Shapiro felt like he wanted to go in a different direction, and I wasn't part of it. I have never left Cleveland because I didn't want to be there—the only reason why I left was because someone else didn't want me there."

John Hart had made a reputation of being unafraid to make blockbuster trades. Mark Shapiro took his approach and made a very risky move on December 11, 2001, when he traded away future Hall of Famer Roberto Alomar to the Mets for Alex Escobar, Matt Lawton, Jerrod Riggan and players to be named later. Escobar was a young talent and seen as the blue chip in the deal. However, his career never got off the ground as numerous injuries kept him from reaching his full potential.

Matt Lawton had had a decent career while playing with the Twins before coming over to the Mets. He was seen as the immediate starter of the bunch and someone who was versatile in the field and could hit anywhere in the lineup. Lawton would join Brady Anderson in the outfield as the Indians searched for the third and final piece.

Opening night in Anaheim against the Angels started off with many of the familiar faces Indians fans had grown to love. On the mound was

Bartolo Colón, while Einar Diaz was behind the plate. Jim Thome still resided at first base, with Omar Vizquel at shortstop and Travis Fryman at third. The outfield looked vastly different, however, with Matt Lawton in right, Russell Branyan in left and new center fielder Milton Bradley rounding out the lineup.

Matt Lawton was held hitless in his first night as a member of the Cleveland Indians; however, the other eight starters, including new second baseman Ricky Gutierrez, each had at least one hit as the Indians rolled along to a 6-0 victory. Colón looked amazing as he tossed a complete-game shutout, allowing only five hits while striking out five batters. It was a positive start to a season that many felt nervous about.

In the second game of the series, Cleveland wasn't nearly as effective, losing 7–5 after a shaky outing by CC Sabathia. However, the Indians bounced back from the loss in epic fashion by rolling off a ten-game winning streak. They swept teams such as the Royals, Tigers and Twins in dominant fashion. Bob Wickman saved four of the ten wins, while Colón, Sabathia and Baez had two wins each during that stretch. The Indians were off to a red-hot start for the first time in many years.

At 11-1, the only thing that could have possibly cooled them off was the weather—and that's exactly what happened on Sunday, April 14, 2002, when their home game against the Kansas City Royals was rained out. With that Monday being an off day, fans and media feared that the two consecutive days off might hurt the team's momentum. The Indians went on to lose six straight after that, getting swept in both Chicago and Minnesota. They managed to stop the skid by beating Chicago at home before losing nine of the next ten. They suddenly went from the hottest team in baseball to a struggling 13-16 team. Things remained shaky, and they finished May with a record of 26-28.

The Indians fell into a June swoon and failed to get back to .500. As June played out and things failed to improve, Shapiro started to make moves that would officially begin the dreaded rebuilding process. On June 7, 2002, the Indians traded Russell Branyan to the Cincinnati Reds for first baseman Ben Broussard. It was a minor trade but one made with a youth movement in mind. Twenty days after the Broussard deal with Cincinnati, Shapiro would strike again in a trade that rocked Cleveland to its core.

On June 27, 2002, the Cleveland Indians traded Bartolo Colón and Tim Drew to the Montreal Expos for Cliff Lee, Brandon Phillips, Grady Sizemore and Lee Stevens. Phillips, a second baseman, was seen as the key piece in the deal. However, it would be prospects Sizemore and Lee who

Bartolo Colón was dealt to the Montreal Expos in a blockbuster trade that shaped Cleveland's future. *Photo by Dr. Gosky.*

developed to be the best players in the deal as the years went on. Sizemore became an excellent and consistent leadoff hitter, while Lee would reach CY Young status in 2008. Colón was 10-4 at the time of the trade and the key starter of the Indians' rotation.

It was a major move that signaled a changing of the times for Cleveland. Gone were the days of loaded lineups and high-priced free agents. The Indians were set to rebuild, and in order to do so, they need to redevelop a young core of players. The players remaining from the glory years were Jim Thome, who was set to be a free agent at the end of the year, and veteran shortstop Omar Vizquel. Travis Fryman was also still on the roster, but he was set to retire at season's end.

The Indians headed into the All Star break with a record of 39-47 and sinking fast. Charlie Manuel, whose contract was up at the end of the season, had a meeting with management to decide on his future with the team. Apparently, Manuel became upset when management wouldn't commit to him long term, and instead of waiting until the end of the season, the team and Charlie decided to part ways then and there. Third base coach and former Indians catcher Joel Skinner would finish the season as interim manager until management could regroup at season's end to formally begin the search for a new skipper.

The Indians' fire sale continued on July 19 when they traded left-handed starter Chuck Finley to St. Louis for a minor leaguer and outfielder Coco Crisp. The season ended a few months later, and it was the worst on record since moving into Jacobs Field. Like with anything in life, there is going to be some growing pains, and the Indians were clearly feeling them as they finished the season at 74-88.

It wasn't all bad, however, as several players put together good seasons. CC Sabathia again had double-digit wins by finishing at 13-11 with a 4.37 ERA. Young hurlers Danys Báez and Ryan Drese finished with ten wins each, and Bob Wickman battled through injury to save twenty games. Sadly, 2002 did spell the end for beloved fan favorite Charles Nagy. It was an injury-plagued season that saw Nagy finish at 1-4 with an 8.88 ERA. Despite the sad end for Nagy, he remains one of the most beloved players to ever wear an Indians jersey.

Jim Thome had his best year as a Cleveland Indian by hitting for a .304 average with a career-high fifty-two home runs. Thome was about to be a free agent, and he was peaking at the right time. Few, if any, fans felt that Thome would leave town the same way in which Ramirez and Belle had years prior.

With the rebuilding mode in full swing, the 2002–03 off-season would be very important. Charles Nagy and Jaret Wright were both granted free agency, with no intention of being resigned; the two key elements of the epic Game 7 of the 1997 World Series would no longer be on the roster. It was another sign that the glory years of the late '90s were over and that the team was focused on the future.

The first move was to hire a new manager to guide the team. On October 29, 2002, Mark Shapiro and Larry Dolan hired Eric Wedge as the thirty-ninth manager of the Cleveland Indians. Wedge had played catcher in the Major Leagues briefly with the Boston Red Sox and Colorado Rockies. He had been managing in the Cleveland farm system since 1998, and they felt he would be the man to lead the Indians back to prominence.

Jim Thome broke the hearts of Cleveland fans everywhere when he signed with Philadelphia on December 6, 2002. Thome was seen as the one free agent who would not leave Cleveland; if anything, people saw him as the type of player to give a team a hometown discount. Sadly, Thome left for the Phillies, who were looking to contend right away and also had moved into a brand-new stadium of their own.

Fan favorite Jim Thome left after the 2002 season. *Photo by Dr. Gosky.*

The 2003 season would prove to be a very challenging one for the Cleveland Indians. They finished with a 68-94 record, and their attendance dropped to twelfth out of fourteen in the American League. Wedge did his best in his first year as manager. The Indians were in the first year of a three-year plan and had to look for bright spots wherever they could find them.

The starting rotation was once again bolstered by CC Sabathia at the top. For the third straight season, Sabathia was able to get double-digit wins, finishing with a record of 13-9. It was crystal clear that he would be the Indians' ace for a very long time. With Wickman sidelined with an injury, Baez was able to step up and save twenty-five games. It was the lone highlight for Baez, who ended the year at 2-9. Cliff Lee won three games in nine starts that season, a sign of things to come.

Young talents such as catcher Victor Martinez, shortstop Jhonny Peralta and first baseman Travis Hafner all cut their teeth with the Indians that season as well. Those names would be prominent in a playoff run only a few short years later. Despite the rough season, the new core of the Indians was slowly taking shape.

The 2004 season revealed the emergence of two new big arms joining CC Sabathia in the rotation. Cliff Lee, who many viewed as a throw-in in the

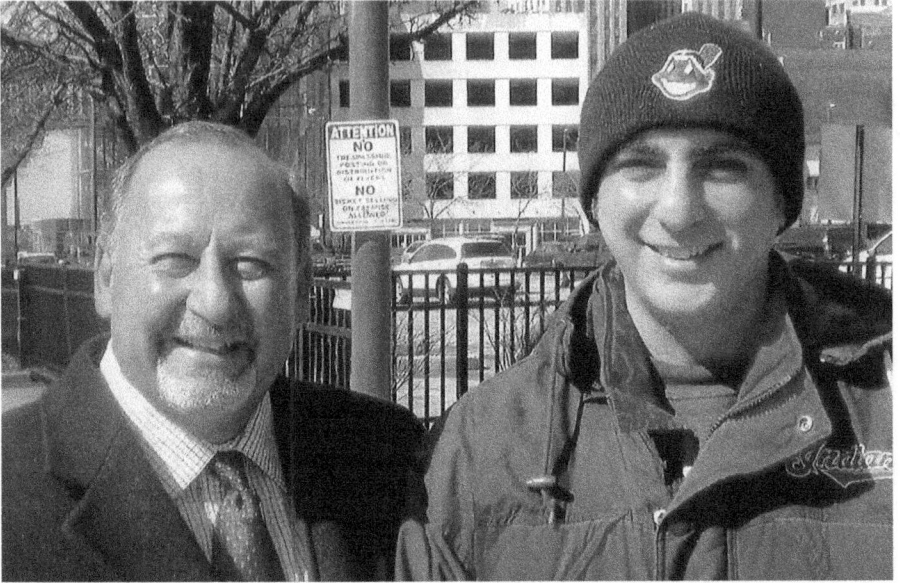

Bobby DiBiasio Sr. (left) is the Indians' vice-president of public affairs. *Photo by Richard Masci.*

Omar Vizquel left after the 2004 season. *Photo by Dr. Gosky.*

Brandon Phillips–Bartolo Colón deal in 2002, had a stellar first season as a full-time member of the rotation. Lee finished with fourteen wins, which was good enough to tie teammate Jake Westbrook for the team lead. Westbrook had a good ERA of 3.38 after joining the rotation early in the season. With Westbrook and Lee playing well, it was staff ace CC Sabathia once again finishing with double-digit wins at 11-10. These three arms would be a key part of the future, and they helped build a starting rotation on which Wedge could rely for a long time to come.

The lineup also improved drastically during the season as several young talents continued to excel and grow. Victor Martinez, a team leader on and off the field, was the anchor behind the plate and captain in the clubhouse. Martinez, who was great for team morale and backed up his attitude with great play on the field, finished with a .283 batting average, twenty-three home runs and 108 RBIs.

Ben Broussard continued to play well at first base, finishing with a .275 batting average, seventeen home runs and 82 RBIs. Broussard was also a key piece in the team's mid-August run, which saw him hit several game-changing home runs that brought the Indians within one game of first-place Minnesota. The Indians had been trailing the Twins all season but had narrowed the lead to one by August 14. They used a six-game winning streak to bring packed houses back to The Jake, but they eventually fell behind the Twins again and closed out the year in third place with a record of 80-82.

Despite missing the playoffs, it was evident that the team was improving and had a bright future. Key free-agent pickup Ronnie Belliard filled his role beautifully as he finished with a team-high forty-eight doubles. Casey Blake finished tied for the team lead with twenty-eight home runs. Travis Hafner also hit twenty-eight home runs, along with batting .311 and driving in 109 runs, on his way to becoming the much-needed power threat in the middle of the lineup.

Mid-season call-up Grady Sizemore showed early signs of sparking the lineup with his speed and crafty defense. In only forty-three games, he knocked in twenty-four RBIs and had four home runs. They were decent numbers but only a mere glimpse of his true potential. Sizemore would become the full-time starting center fielder the following season and go on to be one of the best outfielders in baseball for many years to come.

Perhaps the biggest off-season signing was veteran starting pitcher Kevin Millwood. A key piece of the Atlanta Braves rotation for many years, Millwood was seen as the perfect veteran to guide the improving rotation. Juan Gonzalez was also brought back into the fold, but it wouldn't last long for him as he got hurt in his very first at-bat of the season. The Gonzalez injury proved to be a huge blessing in disguise, however, as it made room in the outfield for Grady Sizemore to become a full-time starter.

With the roster set and hopes high, the Indians took the field for the season opener at new Comiskey Field in Chicago to face the White Sox. Jake Westbrook pitched a gem, going eight innings and giving up only one run on four hits. The opposing starter, Mark Buerhle, was only slightly better, giving up two hits and no runs for the win. It was a tough way to start the season, but once again Westbrook showed that he was improving each and every start.

Game two of the series was similar, with Kevin Millwood tossing another gem. The Indians held a commanding 3–0 lead heading into the bottom of the ninth with Bob Wickman coming in for the save. Wickman completely imploded and proceeded to blow the game, giving up back-to-back home runs by Konerko and Dye after allowing a leadoff single. The home runs tied the game and gave Chicago the momentum. Wickman completed the meltdown by giving up a double to Aaron Rowand, walking A.J. Pierzynski and then committing an error on a Willie Harris bunt back to the mound, loading the bases with only one out. Juan Uribe capped off the White Sox comeback with a sacrifice fly to win the game. It was a frustrating way to start the season; the Indians had played well enough to win twice but had nothing to show for it. The two tough losses caused Cleveland to stumble out of the gate and finish April 9-14.

The Indians showed a ton of heart as they bounced back in May and began playing very well. They finished the month on a four-game winning streak to pull even at 25-25. The problem was that the White Sox were off to one of the hottest starts in the history of baseball, and the Indians trailed by nine games heading into June.

The Indians caught fire in June when it came time to play inter-league ball. They rolled off nine straight wins (and were twelve of thirteen overall), all of them coming against National League teams. The Indians were red hot, and they would need to be to keep pace with the equally hot White Sox. The Indians finished June at 42-35 and eleven games behind Chicago.

The Indians continued to play .500 ball in July and finished the month with a 55-51 record, still 14.5 games back of Chicago. With only two months left in the season, things looked bleak for the Tribe. With the leadership of Eric Wedge and the heart of fierce competitors, the Indians proceeded to go on a furious two-month run that pulled them to within 2.5 games of the White Sox with only 10 games to go.

It was an epic comeback by the Indians and a colossal meltdown by the White Sox. The Indians used solid pitching and timely hitting to make a furious late season push at the playoffs. On Sunday, September 25, 2005, the Indians entered Kaufmann Stadium in Kansas City only 1.5 games back of Chicago. It ended up being the closest the Indians would get, as for the first time all season, they began to show their age. The last week of the season was filled with mistakes and hitting slumps. They lost six of their final seven games and narrowly missed the division and wildcard spot. It was a heartbreaking end to an otherwise stellar season. They finished with ninety-three wins, which in most seasons would be more than enough for a playoff spot. This was just one of those odd years where ninety-three wins did not get your team into October baseball.

As disappointing as missing the playoffs was, the Indians could still hold their heads high as they had played great and pushed one of the best teams in baseball to the limit. The White Sox would eventually win the World Series that season. The final regular-season series against the White Sox brought crowds of more than forty thousand to Jacobs Field each night. It showed once again that when a winning and exciting product is put on the field, the fans will show up in droves.

Travis Hafner had another productive season at the plate by smashing thirty-three home runs and 108 RBIs. Victor Martinez once again showed his ability to be one of the best-hitting catchers in the American League as he hit .305 with twenty home runs and 80 RBIs. Grady Sizemore excelled in his new role as leadoff hitter and everyday center fielder by playing in 158 games and collecting 185 hits. Sizemore also stole twenty-two bases and scored 111 runs, ideal numbers for any leadoff hitter.

The rotation continued to take shape and remained one of the strong points of the team. Cliff Lee looked amazing in an eighteen-win season, while CC Sabathia and Jake Westbrook each chipped in with fifteen wins of their own. The top three in the rotation remained one of the best trios in baseball. Millwood didn't get much run support, which hurt his win total, but the free agent managed to finish the regular season with a razor-thin 2.86 ERA. It was one of the lowest in baseball. Despite blowing his share of saves and looking very shaky in others, Bob Wickman did manage to close out forty-five games. With a run of late season wins and ever-improving talent, things were looking up heading into the 2006 season and beyond.

Chapter 7

# PLAYOFF BASEBALL RETURNS

Expectations for the Indians were high heading into the 2006 season. They had come within one game of making the playoffs the prior season, and the returning core of the team was one of the best young groups in baseball.

The rotation lost a crafty veteran in Kevin Millwood but picked up a solid starter in Paul Byrd on December 7, 2005. Byrd had been in the league for over a decade and would bring much-needed veteran stability to the rotation. He was also coming off a season of double-digit wins for the Angels.

The Indians took the field at U.S. Cellular Field for the season opener against the Chicago White Sox. As the first game of the year, it was televised nationally that Sunday night. The spotlight was on Cleveland, but the light would quickly fade as Sabathia struggled and was knocked out of the game in the third inning. Chicago went on to blow out the Indians by a score of 10–4.

But Eric Wedge had his men ready to bounce back from the opening-night loss, and they crushed Chicago 8–2 the following game. It would be the first of six straight wins for the Indians, who looked as though they had kept the momentum they had gained at the end of the previous season. The rest of the month was shaky, however, and they ended up finishing 13-12. They then suffered a surprising six-game losing streak in mid-May that caused them to stumble through the rest of the month and finish at 26-26 heading into June.

The team endured a horrible June swoon and staggered into July with a subpar record of 35-43. Everyone hoped for a second-half resurgence like

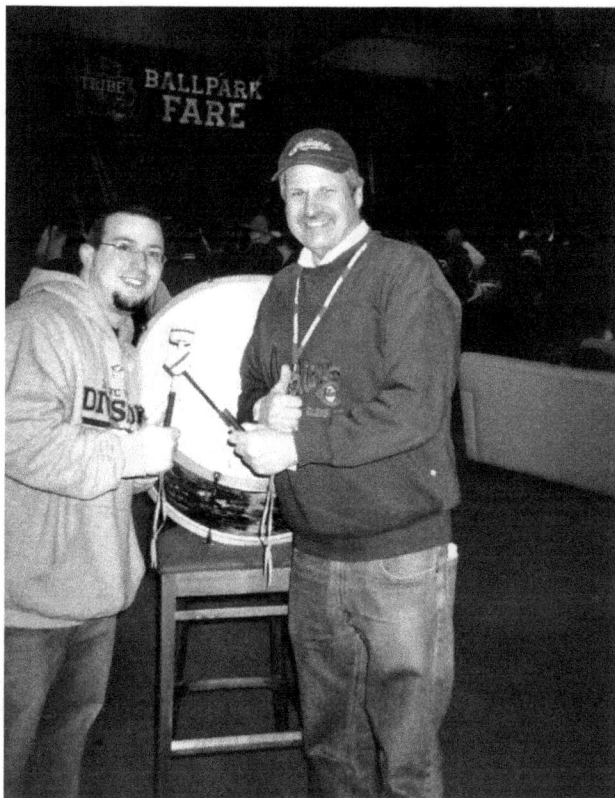

*Left*: John Adams has been beating the drum in the stands for more than thirty years. *Photo by Vince McKee.*

*Below*: Cleveland Indians broadcaster Jim Rosenhaus (second from left). *Photo by Vince McKee.*

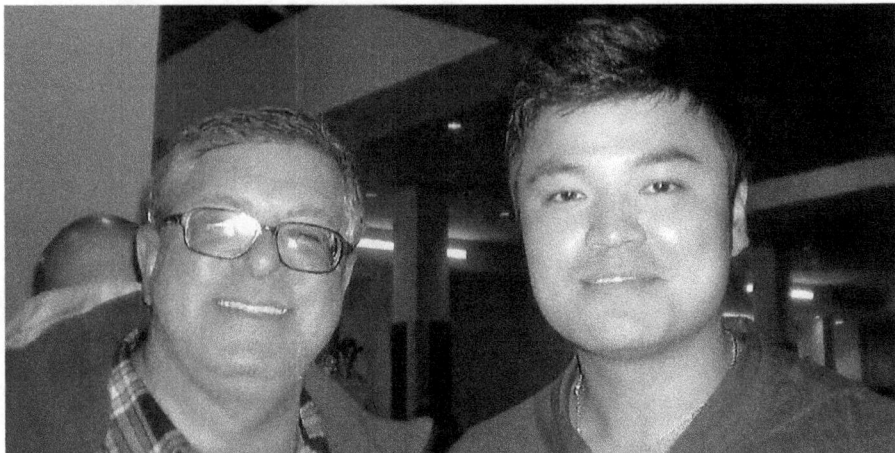

Outfielder Shin-Soo Choo (right) takes time out to meet with a fan. *Photo by Richard Masci.*

that of 2005, but that would not happen, as the Indians never could seem to get back on track.

As the playoffs seemed further out of reach, the Indians once again started making moves to build for the future. They signed amateur free-agent pitcher Danny Salazar and traded Eduardo Perez to Seattle for highly touted infield prospect Asdrubal Cabrera. It was a trade that would eventually pay off highly as Cabrera would become a reliable piece of the middle infield for several years afterward. Cleveland made another trade with Seattle a short while later, sending Ben Broussard to the Mariners for outfielder Shin-Soo Choo.

The Indians finished the year in fourth place at 78-84. It was a disappointing season that had begun with high hopes. There was a silver lining in this dark cloud, however, as several players had outstanding seasons. Despite missing some time due to injury, Sabathia went 12-11, reaching double-digit wins for the sixth straight season. Cliff Lee demonstrated sharp command of his pitches and continued to impress, winning fourteen games while striking out 129 batters and walking only 58. Jake Westbrook, who arose from the bullpen to become a full-time starter in 2004, had another outstanding season, leading the team in wins at 15-10.

Paul Byrd had a disappointing first season with the Indians as he went a mediocre 10-9. Rafael Betancourt had emerged as a solid eighth-inning setup man, but the Indians would need to find someone for him to set up, as Bob Wickman had been traded at mid-season.

Several key players in the starting lineup once again had great seasons. Victor Martinez continued to establish himself as one of the best-hitting catchers in the game by batting .316 with sixteen home runs and 93 RBIs. Grady Sizemore had a productive season as the leadoff man by hitting .290, stealing twenty-two bases and playing in all 162 games. He also led the team with fifty-three doubles. Travis Hafner continued to flex his power over opposing pitchers by crushing forty-two home runs and knocking in 117 RBIs. Once again, the Indians had the key pieces in place and were set to make a run at the division in 2007.

The off-season presented new challenges for general manger Mark Shapiro. It had been awhile since he needed a closer, but the mid-season departure of Bob Wickman created a hole at the back end of the bullpen. On December 6, 2006, Shapiro signed Joe Borowski from the Florida Marlins to be the new closer. Borowski was a veteran who had already played on seven teams in his twelve-year career. He still had good stuff, though, and the Indians brass felt he was the right man for the job.

Second-year pitcher Fausto Carmona was brought into the rotation to start the season. He had dabbled in a few bullpen roles in 2006 but never found his niche. He had great stuff, and manager Eric Wedge felt that he could be a viable starter to go along with Sabathia, Westbrook and Lee.

The Indians started off the season by winning their opening game on the road against the White Sox and taking two out of three in the series. They returned to Cleveland for the home opener against the Seattle Mariners, who were now managed by former Indians skipper Mike Hargrove. The spirits and emotions of the fans were high for the game; however, the weather was unable to cooperate. The Indians had a lead going into the top of the fifth, but the snow was starting to fall harder. Mike Hargrove argued with the umpires just long enough for the weather to worsen to the point that the game had to be postponed. The Indians had needed only one more out for the game to be official before it was called.

The weather failed to improve, so the following series against the Angels was relocated to Miller Park in Milwaukee. The three-game series averaged an attendance of 17,498. Fans packed Miller Park for the chance to see two American League teams that normally only play in Milwaukee during inter-league play.

The Indians won game one of the series, thanks to a superb outing from CC Sabathia. New Indians closer Joe Borowski held on in the ninth inning to give the Indians the 7–6 victory. Angels pitcher Joe Saunders dominated the second game, and the Angels won 4–1. The Indians took the rubber match, thanks in part to a mammoth three-run home run from Travis Hafner.

The Indians continued to have a solid first month despite all the weather and stadium issues they had been forced to deal with. They finished the month of April with a 14-8 record, having won seven of their last eight games. They were picking up steam at the right time.

The Indians swept the Blue Jays to start May and carried that momentum with them. Later in the month, they returned to Jacobs Field, where they went 6-1 against the Twins, Mariners, and Reds. Despite a series loss to the Royals at Kaufmann Stadium, they swept the contending Tigers in Detroit, helping them finish the month 19-11. They closed out May with an overall record of 33-19, three and a half games ahead of second place in the division.

June was a bit of an up-and-down month for the Indians, but they finished the month with an impressive overall record of 48-32 and remained in first place by 1.5 games. As the All Star Game approached, Cleveland fans were excited to learn that three players would be making their way to the Midsummer Classic. Victor Martinez, Grady Sizemore and CC Sabathia were all elected to play in that year's game. Shapiro had traded for Sizemore years prior in the Colón deal and was now reaping the benefits.

One very pleasant surprise for the Indians was second-year pitcher Fausto Carmona. Many were unsure of how he would perform in his first year as part of the full-time rotation, but the promotion from the bullpen paid off as Carmona headed into the All Star break with a record of 10-4 and 3.85 ERA. His emergence couldn't have come at a better time as usual reliable starter Cliff Lee was struggling. Lee was getting roughed up and couldn't find his command. He closed out July with a 5-8 record and a ballooning 6.38 ERA. CC Sabathia remained hot as the ace of the staff, leading the team into the final two months of the season with a 13-6 record.

It was during this stretch that Wedge decided to bench second baseman Josh Barfield for rookie Asdrubal Cabrera. "A-Cab" had the hot hand and glove as the Indians looked to continue chasing another division crown. It would be their first since 2001 if they could close it out. It was also during this time that they traded for fan favorite and longtime Indians veteran Kenny Lofton, sending Hector Luna to the Texas Rangers in exchange. Lofton expresses some of the emotions he had coming back to Cleveland: "Cleveland was a place where I felt comfortable and wanted to be. I welcomed the opportunity to come back to Cleveland with open arms. I felt like this was the place I should have been in the first place. I felt like it was time for me to come back. I told the Rangers that I would love to be traded to Cleveland. The situation worked out pretty good as we had the chance to go to the playoffs. We made

Kenny Lofton returned to the team for the 2007 playoff run. *Photo by Kim Murphy*.

it to within one game of going back to the World Series. I enjoyed my time coming back—it was fun."

With Lofton back in prime form and the rest of the lineup continuing to surge, the Indians rolled through the last two months of the season and finished in first place. Their final record was 96-66, the most wins in a season in nearly eight years.

Leading the staff was Cy Young winner CC Sabathia, who had a 19-7 record to go along with a 3.21 ERA. Every bit as impressive was his teammate Fausto Carmona, who also won nineteen games and had an even lower ERA of 3.06. Veteran Paul Byrd also returned to form, chipping in with fifteen wins. Joe Borowski did great in his first season as Indians closer as he successfully converted forty-five saves.

New first baseman Ryan Garko played well in his first season as a full-time starter, finishing with twenty-one home runs and 61 RBIs. Victor Martinez once again had a sensational season, batting .301 with twenty-five home runs and 114 RBIs. Martinez was starting to make his name as the premier catcher in the American League. Grady Sizemore again played in all 162 games and stole thirty-three bases while doing it. Sizemore also hit twenty-four home runs, scored a team-high 118 runs and showed incredible discipline at the plate, drawing 101 walks. It was a mark surpassed only by teammate Travis Hafner, who had 102 walks to go along with his twenty-four home runs and 100 RBIs. Franklin Gutierrez proved to be a great threat off the bench, hitting .266 with thirteen home runs. He also provided solid defense late in games.

The first round presented a matchup with the New York Yankees. CC Sabathia took the mound for Game 1 against the powerful Yankee lineup. Johnny Damon started things off with a bang by hitting a home run off of Sabathia in the first at-bat of the game. It was a stunning way to start the game, but Sabathia bounced back and got out of the inning without giving up any more runs.

The Indians wasted no time in responding against Yankee pitcher Chien-Ming Wang in the bottom half of the first. A two-run single by Ryan Garko was followed by an RBI single from Lofton to put the Indians ahead 3–1. Sabathia settled down and kept the lead heading into the bottom of the third. A leadoff home run by Asdrubal Cabrera widened the Indians' lead to 4–1. A Robinson Cano home run in the top of the fourth brought the Yankees back to within two.

A Bobby Abreu RBI double in the top of the fifth shortened the lead to 4–3; however, in the bottom half of the fifth, the Indians exploded for five runs. The inning was highlighted by a two-run home run by Victor Martinez, a two-run double by Casey Blake and a Kenny Lofton RBI single. Suddenly, the Indians held a commanding 9–3 lead going into the sixth.

An inning later, a Travis Hafner home run and a Kenny Lofton RBI double put the game out of reach at 11–3. Later in the game, Ryan Garko polished off the Yankees with a solo home run. The Indians looked dominant in the 12–3 blowout. In his first playoff game with the team since 2001, Lofton had driven in four runs.

Andy Pettitte and Fausto Carmona thrilled the Jacobs Field crowd with a Game 2 pitchers' duel. The Yankees scored once in the third but were held scoreless the rest of the night. It looked like the one run would be enough for the Yankees until late in the night. In the bottom of the eighth, Yankees pitcher Joba Chamberlain was riled up—but not by Indians hitters. He was swarmed with midges. It was one of the rare nights on the lakefront that the tiny winged creatures made their presence felt. A distracted Chamberlain threw a wild pitch to Victor Martinez, allowing the speedy Sizemore to score from third base and tie the game.

The Indians bullpen looked sharp and kept the Yankee batters at bay. Left-handed relief pitcher Rafael Perez looked incredible as he mowed down countless Yankee hitters. Luis Vizcaino took the mound in the bottom of the eleventh desperately trying to keep the game tied. The Indians had a different idea, however, as Lofton walked to start the inning and then advanced to second on a Gutierrez single. Casey Blake did a masterful job bunting Lofton over to third base with only one out. Grady Sizemore drew the intentional walk to load the bases. Two batters later, Travis Hafner singled in Lofton from third, winning the game 2–1 in thrilling fashion.

Game 3 took place in Yankee Stadium as the Indians looked to sweep the series. The Yankees managed to avoid elimination by overcoming an early three-run deficit to hit Jake Westbrook hard. The Yankees knocked Westbrook and the Indians bullpen all over the yard en route to an 8–4 victory.

The Indians called on veteran pitcher Paul Byrd to close things out in Game 4. Byrd's teammates helped out by scoring six times in the first four innings of the game. Grady Sizemore set the table in the very first at-bat of the game by hitting a home run off of Chien-Ming Wang. The Indians managed to make the six runs stand and held on for the win 6–4. They were returning to the American League Championship Series for the first time since 1998.

Waiting in the ALCS was a familiar playoff foe: the Boston Red Sox. Boston was a heavy favorite in the series and wasted no time showing the nation why. In Game 1, the Red Sox crushed CC Sabathia and the Indians 10–3 in front of a packed house at Fenway Park. Josh Beckett looked dominant throughout, and the Red Sox were able to cruise to victory.

Game 2 was an eleven-inning thriller that saw numerous lead changes. Curt Schilling and Fausto Carmona both got hit hard early, and the score was tied 6–6 after six innings of play. The Indians used home runs by Jhonny Peralta and Grady Sizemore to do the bulk of their damage. The Red Sox scored on big home runs by Manny Ramirez and Mike Lowell. Both lineups were red hot on a cold October night at Fenway Park.

The scoring spree suddenly stopped as both bullpens shut down the opposing hitters. The game remained tied heading into the eleventh inning. Eric Gagne replaced Boston closer Jonathan Papelbon to start the inning. Gagne struck out Casey Blake before giving up a single to Sizemore and walking Cabrera. Javier Lopez came in to replace Gagne, but he couldn't hold the Indians bats at bay as Trot Nixon singled, scoring Sizemore from the third. A wild pitch to Martinez followed by hits from Garko and Peralta put the Indians ahead 10–6. Franklin Gutierrez put the Red Sox away for good by crushing a three-run home run and extending the lead to 13–6. The Indians held on and won Game 2 by that same score.

The Indians returned home for the next three games of the series. They won Games 3 and 4, thanks to great pitching efforts by Jake Westbrook and Paul Byrd. The one-time underdog was now up 3-1 in the series and had people around baseball talking about a giant upset. Cleveland would not close things out on its home field, however, as Josh Beckett once again shut down the Indians lineup in Game 5 and sent the series back to Boston.

Fausto Carmona got beaten badly again in Game 6 at Fenway. Although he had looked great in the divisional series against the Yankees, he had clearly run out of gas. The Red Sox jumped on him early and often en route to a 12–2 blowout. The series was headed for a dramatic Game 7.

Taking the mound for Game 7 for the Indians would be Jake Westbrook. The normally reliable Westbrook was coming off of an injury-plagued season and looking to erase the memories of a rough regular season. Opposing Westbrook was Boston Red Sox pitcher Daisuke Matsuzaka.

The Red Sox wasted no time in jumping all over Westbrook by scoring a run in each of the first three innings. Manny Ramirez continued to have a huge series by driving in the first of those three runs. Westbrook was able to settle down and hold the Red Sox in check from there as the Indians slowly started to make a comeback. They were able to score single runs in both the fourth and fifth innings to narrow the gap to 3–2.

After a scoreless sixth inning from both teams, the Indians looked to get back on the board when Lofton reached second base on a one-out error by Boston. Franklin Gutierrez followed with a single to left field off Boston reliever Hideki Okajima. The ball was clearly deep enough to score Lofton from second base; however, in a stunning move, Joel Skinner gave Lofton the stop sign at third base. It was infuriating for Indians fans, as Skinner's blunder ended up taking away the run that would have tied the game. The following batter, Casey Blake, hit into a double play and left Lofton stranded. The score remained 3–2 in favor of the Red Sox, and the move by Joel Skinner is still questioned years later. Kenny Lofton shares his thoughts on the controversial play: "I had no idea what was going on behind me. When I finally looked up after being stopped, I saw that the ball was still in the outfield and hadn't even been fielded yet. I could have been home and in the dugout doing high-fives with teammates before the ball would have ever crossed the plate."

The Indians would never recover from the costly decision by Skinner. The Red Sox seized control in the bottom half of the inning and scored two more times to improve their lead to 5–2. They piled on six more runs in the eighth inning, and the celebration was on in Fenway. For the Indians and their fans, it was a painful way to end the season.

The aftereffects of the epic 3–1 collapse were felt for a very long time, as the Indians would fail to return to the playoffs the following season. The 2008 campaign also saw the trade of 2007 Cy Young award winner and Indians homegrown star CC Sabathia. Mark Shapiro was not going to let another free agent leave at the end of the season without getting something for him.

Jacobs Field became Progressive Field in 2008. *Photo by Vince McKee.*

Cliff Lee won the 2008 American League Cy Young award. *Courtesy of LaNasas Barbershop.*

Shapiro pulled the trigger on the deal to send Sabathia to the Milwaukee Brewers for Matt Laporta, Rob Bryson, Zach Johnson and Michael Brantley. While Laporta was the key piece in the deal, it was Brantley who went on to become a reliable member of the Indians lineup for many years after. Brantley performed well in any spot in the batting order and also showed his versatility by being able to play all three outfield positions.

A few weeks later, Shapiro made another good trade when he sent away strikeout-prone third baseman Casey Blake to the Los Angeles Dodgers for minor-league All Star catcher Carlos Santana. Shapiro was shaping the team nicely for the future, as weeks prior he had drafted standout prospect Lonnie Chisenhall. As the Indians struggled through the current season, it was Shapiro placing the building blocks for a bright future.

The Indians finished the 2008 season with an 81-81 record. For the second straight year, the Cy Young award came to Cleveland, this time awarded to twenty-game winner Cliff Lee. Lee looked amazing as he went an outstanding 22-3 with a razor-thin 2.54 ERA. Lee was incredible all season and gave the Indians hope for 2009.

Sadly for the Indians and their fans, however, the 2009 season started off horribly and never got any better. Once again, the Indians fell victim to Eric Wedge's trademark slow start, losing their first five games and also their first seven out of eight. Wedge could never get it turned around, and the Indians ended up losing a depressing ninety-seven games.

Mark Shapiro knew he had to keep acquiring pieces for the future via trades and the draft. One key draft pick was Jason Kipnis, who was selected in the second round of the amateur draft. Kipnis would soon become the full-time second baseman for the Indians and was named to the All Star team in 2013.

For the second straight season, the Indians were forced to part with another Cy Young award winner in Cliff Lee, who was dealt to the Philadelphia Phillies for prime pitching prospects Carlos Carrasco and Jason Knapp. Perhaps the most painful trade Shapiro had to make—but also the most productive—was the deal that sent clubhouse favorite and team leader Victor Martinez to the Red Sox for pitcher Justin Masterson. The Red Sox had Martinez for only a short period of time before he signed as a free agent with the Tigers. Meanwhile, Masterson would become the ace of the Indians rotation just a few seasons later.

It was a rough season but one that was filled with moves that would help the team in the long term. Eric Wedge was eventually let go after the 65-97 season. He had a good run in Cleveland, but now it was time for the next act(a).

Chapter 8

# THE NEXT ACT(A)

Since the Indians had moved to Jacobs Field, each manager had taken his team to the playoffs at least once. That would be the goal for new manager Manny Acta, who was set to take over for the 2010 season. Acta had managed the Washington Nationals for a few subpar seasons, but Indians management felt that he would do better with superior talent. The 2010 season would be the last for Mark Shapiro as general manager, as he was set to take over the role of president at season's end. He wanted his last hire as general manager to be a good one.

The 2010 preseason was quiet; with the exception of a new manager, there weren't many changes or additions. The Indians did bring in Shelley Duncan and Austin Kearns to platoon in the outfield and add some much-needed power to the lineup.

The Tribe got off to a slow start, and as the trade deadline approached, it was apparent that the playoffs would not be possible. Once again, the Indians front office began making moves for the future of the team, trading Austin Kearns to the New York Yankees for minor-league starting pitcher Zach McAllister. It was seen as a minor move at the time; however, McAllister would become a key member of the rotation only a few short seasons later. Another important trade saw Jake Westbrook dealt to the St. Louis Cardinals. As part of the three-team deal, the Indians received minor-league starting pitcher Corey Kluber. Much like the McAllister deal, the move would pay off only a few years later, when Kluber became a viable threat in the starting rotation.

It was a season of growing pains as Cleveland finished 69-93, taking fourth in the division. It was also a season riddled with injuries for several key members of the team. Grady Sizemore played in only thirty-three games due to chronic knee issues. The team's best power hitter, Travis Hafner, also missed plenty of time due to injuries. Both players would continue to battle injuries for the remainder of their Cleveland careers.

One bright spot was the play of new reliever Chris Perez, who was able to save twenty-three games in his first season as the Indians' full-time closer. Perez helped solidify the back end of the bullpen, as Joe Smith and Tony Sipp began to excel in their roles as setup men. Starting pitchers Justin Masterson and Josh Tomlin also played well and would be counted on the following season.

The 2011 season would be the first under new general manager Chris Antonetti, who had worked with the Cleveland Indians since 1999. Antonetti had worked closely with Mark Shapiro and was the perfect man for the job.

Antonetti's first move was to bring in veteran third baseman Jack Hannahan. Hannahan was sharp with the glove and looked to hold down the job until hot prospect Lonnie Chisenhall was ready to take over. Antonetti was not done bringing in free agents yet, however, as he also signed veteran infielder Orlando Cabrera in hopes of strengthening the hole at second base and also providing leadership in the clubhouse.

Cleveland Indians catcher Carlos Santana in the clubhouse with sportswriter Vince McKee. *Photo by V Peter Press.*

The 2011 season began on a sour note with a 15–10 loss to the Chicago White Sox. The Indians had trailed 14–0 early but battled back to make it a much closer game, only to fall short in the end. Their spirits didn't stay down for long, however, as they bounced back from the Opening Day loss to win eight of their next nine games. The hot start was due to strong starting pitching and timely two-out hitting. The buzz was returning to Jacobs Field, and fans started filling the

*Left*: Chris Antonetti took over the GM position from Mark Shapiro to start the 2011 season. *Photo by Richard Masci.*

*Below*: Curtis Danburg, senior director of communications, with sportswriter Vince McKee. *Photo by V Peter Press.*

stands to get a glance at the first-place team. The Indians remained hot and finished the first quarter of the season with a 30-15 record.

The hot start saw several of the Indians' young prospects emerge into solid full-time starters. Carlos Santana reveled in his role behind the plate and was a strong bat in the middle of the lineup. Asdrubal Cabrera remained a fast glove at shortstop and another hitter whom Acta could count on at the top of the order. With Grady Sizemore out with injury, Michael Brantley stepped up and provided a spark with both his bat and his glove. It was clear that Brantley was the key piece in the CC Sabathia trade.

As the season went on, the team hit a June swoon that saw their record drop to 42-37. However, they were still in the thick of the divisional race with the Detroit Tigers. In mid-season, Jason Kipnis was called up from the minors and quickly caught fire as a member of the big-league club. Kipnis, who had a great bat and the ability to provide a spark when needed, fit in right away and quickly took the starting second base position away from Orlando Cabrera. His ever-improving defensive skills led to a healthy double play combination with Asdrubal Cabrera.

Then, with the trade deadline only minutes away and the Indians playing .500 ball (53-52), general manger Chris Antonetti pulled the trigger on a blockbuster deal. The Indians traded away their two biggest pitching prospects—Drew Pomeranz and Alex White—to the Colorado Rockies for ace starter Ubaldo Jimenez. It was a risky trade that had the potential for a huge payoff. Antonetti showed he had the guts to make moves that would provide the instant impact needed by a team in the pennant race.

Ubaldo Jimenez had had an incredible 2010 season with the Colorado Rockies—good enough to earn him the role of starting pitcher for the National League in that season's All Star Game. Jimenez had struggled since then, but the Indians brass believed a change of scenery would revive his early 2010 dominance.

Pitcher Josh Tomlin. *Photo by Richard Masci.*

Pitcher Ubaldo Jimenez. *Photo by Richard Masci.*

The hot dog race is a fan favorite at every home game. *Photo by V Peter Press.*

Jim Thome returned to town in a late season move, and it was great for fans to see the return of a past hero. Thome reflects on his return to the Indians: "It was very nice to come home. The first team you sign with always carries a special place with in your heart even if you have to leave. My heart stayed in Cleveland, and it was nice to return."

The Indians continued to play .500 baseball the rest of the season, but it just wasn't good enough to chase down the red-hot Detroit Tigers. They finished the season with an 80-82 record. It was the best record in years, and it had the fans' hopes high for 2012.

Despite missing the playoffs for the fourth consecutive season, there were several bright spots. Carlos Santana finished with twenty-seven home runs and 79 RBIs. It was his first year back from a painful season-ending ankle injury, and played well. Asdrubal Cabrera chipped in with an impressive twenty-five home runs and 92 RBIs.

Justin Masterson emerged as a viable number-one starter in the rotation by winning twelve games and finishing with a low ERA of 3.21. Josh Tomlin also won twelve games and showed tremendous control by allowing only twenty-one walks. Both arms would be crucial to the future success of the team.

While the Indians were getting better on the field, the organization continued to improve the overall fan experience. One highlight includes the annual Rock 'n Blast that occurs every summer. An amazing display of fireworks and music, it has drawn a sellout crowd every season since its inception. The Terrace Club in the left-field stands continues to play host to wedding receptions, company office parties and other major social events. Cleveland Indians Charities also continues to do everything possible to reach out and help people and organizations across the city. If a fan feels like brushing up on his Indians history, he can visit Heritage Park, located just beyond the center field wall. It is a beautiful monument dedicated to everyone who has been inducted into the Indians Hall of Fame. All this, combined with Dollar Dog Nights and Kids Fun Days, where children can run the bases, makes an incredible experience for the entire family. And with great men like Curtis Danburg and Bobby Dibiasio in the Indians front office, bigger and better things are sure to be on the way very soon.

Even Mickey Mouse is a huge Indians fan!
*Photo by Vince McKee.*

The 2012 season began with a lot of hope from Cleveland Indians fans because of the improved play on the field the prior year. Jason Kipnis would be the starting second baseman from the onset. That factor alone was an upgrade from the 2011 season, in which he had been a mid-season call-up.

The Indians used a hot start by recently added veteran starting pitcher Derek Lowe to jump out to an early lead in the Central Division. On June 22, 2012, they were in first place with a 32-27 record. Then they hit the dreaded June swoon and stumbled into the All Star break with a record of 44-41, three games back of the first-place Detroit Tigers.

Cleveland managed to stay in the hunt until late July, when the losing streaks began. The Indians lost eleven in a row, followed by another nine-

*Left*: Carlos Baerga, pictured here with the author, was inducted into the 2013 Cleveland Indians Hall of Fame. *Photo by V Peter Press.*

*Below*: The Rock 'n Blast is a big hit with Indians fans. *Photo by Vince McKee.*

game losing streak in mid-August. Their troubles weren't over yet, however, as they would endure another seven-game losing streak before the end of the month. It was a brutal month that cost Manny Acta his job before the end of the season.

The Indians needed to bring in veteran free agents to guide their young talent. They also needed a proper manager with a big enough name and championship experience to attract those free agents. They made the perfect move on October 6, 2012, when they hired Terry Francona as manager. Francona was considered the key in getting the Indians back to the promised land.

Chapter 9

# THE RETURN TO PROMINENCE

Terry Francona is the son of former Major League ballplayer Tito Francona. Terry grew up watching his dad play while dreaming of his own big-league career. The elder Francona played for the Indians from 1958 through 1964. It was only natural that Terry would bring the Francona name back to Cleveland.

Terry Francona excelled in college, where his University of Arizona team won the 1980 College World Series. Francona was drafted by the Montreal Expos in 1980 and was quickly promoted to the big-league roster. Francona's future as a Major Leaguer looked promising until injuries cut short his career. He even spent a short stint as a Cleveland Indian in 1988 before eventually retiring in 1990.

But Terry Francona has baseball in his blood, and he followed his passion for the game to the managerial ranks when he took over as manager for the Philadelphia Phillies to begin the 1997 season. He spent four hotly contested seasons at the helm before exiting after the 2000 campaign. He gave managing another attempt when he was hired by the Boston Red Sox in 2004. The second time proved to be the charm as he led the Red Sox to their first World Series title since selling Babe Ruth in the early 1900s. Many fans and media felt Boston was cursed, but it took Francona only one season at the helm to lift the curse and bring a World Series title back to Beantown. Francona proved it wasn't a fluke when he did it again in 2007.

Because of ownership issues, Francona left Boston after the 2011 season and spent time in the broadcast booth for *ESPN Sunday Night Baseball*. Terry

*Left*: Terry Francona.
*Courtesy of SammySoso.com.*

*Below*: Jason Giambi was
a team leader for the
Indians in 2013. *Photo by
Richard Masci.*

was a hot commodity as the 2012 off-season began. The Indians were seen by many as long shots to land Francona. But team president Mark Shapiro and general manager Chris Antonetti helped convince Francona that managing in Cleveland was the perfect choice.

With Francona in place, Cleveland suddenly became the top choice for many veteran free agents, who valued his leadership and World Series experience. The Indians promptly signed veteran power hitter Jason Giambi. It was seen as a low-risk, high-reward move as Giambi would bring a great veteran presence and leadership to the clubhouse. Scott Kazmir, a one-time ace in the Tampa

Rays' rotation, signed with Cleveland as well. Kazmir had Cy Young skills and was ready to reclaim his All Star status as a member of the Indians.

But general manager Chris Antonetti wasn't done, as he worked out another great deal with the Cincinnati Reds and Arizona Diamondbacks. The Indians received speedy outfielder Drew Stubbs along with big-name minor-league pitching prospect Trevor Bauer. They had to let go of struggling setup man Tony Sipp and soon-to-be free agent Shin-Shoo Choo. It was another brilliant move by Antonetti to unload a soon-to-be free agent for a player who could help and another player who had ace potential.

Chris Antonetti delivered Cleveland fans a late holiday gift when he brought in big-name free agent Nick Swisher, who had been a stud with the Yankees and brought Word Series experience with him. Swisher has an incredible personality and is beloved by his teammates and fans for his enthusiasm and team spirit. It was the leadership of Swisher that would play a key factor in the 2013 run to the playoffs.

The free-agent season wasn't over with yet, as Antonetti continued to spend wisely by signing power-hitting outfielder Ryan Rayburn. Rayburn was a great backup outfielder who could add some serious pop to the lineup. The Rayburn signing went nicely with the prior free-agent signing of power hitter Mark Reynolds. The Indians lineup suddenly packed a punch!

The last—but certainty not least—piece of the puzzle was added when the Indians signed speedy leadoff hitter Michael Bourne. He was the ideal center fielder, and along with Stubbs and Brantley, the Indians now had the fastest outfield in baseball.

The Indians were loaded headed into the 2013 season, and they had fans and media around baseball talking. The rotation boasted strong arms such as Justin Masterson, Ubaldo Jimenez, Zach McAllister, Corey Kluber and Scott Kazmir.

The Indians used a six-game winning streak at the end of April and the beginning of May to push their record to 14-13. It was taking some time for the new pieces to gel, but Francona stayed the course and was able to keep things on track. By the end of May, the Indians were 29-25 and improving daily. Sadly, they fell victim to the June swoon for the third straight year and lost eight consecutive games to start the month. However, Francona showed exactly why the team had hired him, bringing the Indians back from disaster and leading them to win their next nine of eleven games. They entered the All Star break on a four-game winning streak and a solid record of 51-44, and Jason Kipnis and Justin Masterson represented the team in the Midsummer Classic.

The sold-out crowd was excited for the 2013 home opener against the Yankees. *Photo by V Peter Press.*

The Indians remained hot after the break as they rolled off another eight-game winning streak. They were winning in last-at-bat fashion with a different player assuming the role of hero each night. The magic was returning to Jacobs Field. The Indians finished July with a 59-48 record and were a serious threat to take the division title from Detroit.

However, Cleveland hit a rough part in its schedule and took a small step back in August before entering the final month of the season at 71-64. Once again, the Francona-led Indians showed they could play their best baseball with their backs against the wall. The Indians were amazing in September and used an incredible ten-game winning streak to finish at 92-70, making the playoffs as the first wildcard team. The twenty-one-win month proved that the Indians were for real and that the brightest of times were still to come for Cleveland.

One of several key elements in the late season run was the excellent play of Yan Gomes. Gomes didn't begin the season on the Major League roster, but he used a Lou Marson injury to take over at catcher and played so well that the team couldn't possibly send him back down to Columbus. Gomes made the most of his opportunity and gave the Indians a solid glove and a great arm behind the plate. Jason Kipnis also remained hot as he led the

Playoff baseball returned to The Jake in 2013. *Photo by V Peter Press.*

team with 160 hits and 84 RBIs. Michael Brantley continued to improve into one of the best young outfielders in the game, ending the season with 158 hits, ten home runs and 73 RBIs. Michael Bourne proved to be the perfect leadoff hitter, swiping twenty-three bases and scoring seventy-five runs. Free-agent slugger Nick Swisher led the team with twenty-two home runs and continued to be the spark it needed on the field and in the clubhouse.

The pitching also excelled, with young phenom Danny Salazar taking the league by storm. Salazar nearly pitched a no-hitter in his Major League debut, and finished the season with sixty-five strikeouts in only ten games. He will be a force for a very long time. Perhaps the biggest bright spot was Ubaldo Jimenez, who finally reached the potential seen in him by Indians management. Jimenez had an amazing second half of the season and finished with a team-low 3.30 ERA and thirteen wins. Masterson led the club in wins again with fourteen despite missing several games due to injury. Scott Kazmir also pitched up to prime form, earning ten wins. Corey Kluber, who looked untouchable at times, had his best season by chipping in with eleven wins. Despite the one-game playoff loss to Tampa Bay, one thing was for sure: winning baseball had returned to Cleveland!

# INDEX

# ABOUT THE AUTHOR

Vince McKee is a growing force in the sports literary world. His first two books, *Hero* and *Cleveland's Finest*, exploded onto the Amazon bestsellers list on release. He is the lead writer for www.vpeterpress.com. Vince currently travels the country meeting with the public to spread the message of *Hero*. He is an avid Cleveland sports fan and enjoys spending time with his wife, Emily, and daughter, Maggie. Vince is always willing to speak with his fans and critics and can be contacted at coachvin14@yahoo.com. You can also follow him on twitter @ VinceTheAuthor. This work is the latest in what is sure to be a long career in sports writing for one of Cleveland's finest.

www.ingramcontent.com/pod-product-compliance
Lightning Source LLC
Chambersburg PA
CBHW060810100426
42813CB00004B/1012